More Praise for *Red-Hot Cold Call Selling, Second Edition*

"*Red-Hot Cold-Call Selling* provides insight to effective prospecting, and gives the reader a formula that will improve the success of any salesperson."

   —Susan Levy, Director of Systems Technology Group
      Skills Training, IBM

"*Red-Hot Cold Call Selling* was cutting edge when it was first released in 1995. Now, Paul has established a new standard in prospecting and new business development with the release of the second edition of the book!"

   —Peter McKeon, Managing Director, Salesmasters International

"Many people perceive prospecting and cold calling as a negative aspect of the sales process. Paul brings an incredible level of professionalism and thought-leadership to a never-ending requirement in sales."

   —Jim Rohn, author, *7 Strategies for Wealth and Happiness* and
      The Art of Exceptional Living

"*Red-Hot Cold Call Selling* is an excellent resource for all salespeople from the novice to the experienced professional. It serves as a meaningful guide to help you organize and manage the sales process as well as your time in order to enhance performance and increase results."

   —Harvey Rosenfeld, President, USA Group, Inc.

RED-HOT
COLD CALL
SELLING

Second Edition

Prospecting Techniques That
Really Pay Off

Paul S. Goldner

AMACOM
American Management Association
New York • Atlanta • Brussels • Chicago • Mexico City • San Francisco
Shanghai • Tokyo • Toronto • Washington, D.C.

Special discounts on bulk quantities of AMACOM books are
available to corporations, professional associations, and other
organizations. For details, contact Special Sales Department,
AMACOM, a division of American Management Association,
1601 Broadway, New York, NY 10019.
Tel.: 212-903-8316. Fax: 212-903-8083.
Web site: www.amacombooks.org

This publication is designed to provide accurate and authoritative
information in regard to the subject matter covered. It is sold with the
understanding that the publisher is not engaged in rendering legal,
accounting, or other professional service. If legal advice or other expert
assistance is required, the services of a competent professional person
should be sought.

Library of Congress Cataloging-in-Publication Data

Goldner, Paul S.
    Red-hot cold call selling : prospecting techniques that really pay off / Paul S.
Goldner.—2nd ed.
      p. cm.
    Includes bibliographical references and index.
    ISBN-10: 0-8144-7348-2
    ISBN-13: 978-0-8144-7348-1
    1. Telephone selling.   2. Selling.   I. Title.

  HF5438.3.G647   2006
  658.8'72—dc22

                                          2005036

Printing number

10 9 8 7 6 5 4 3 2

To the two great girls in my life:
Jacqueline
and
Elissa

Contents

Preface

A lot has changed in the 10 years since I wrote this book.

Technology has become quite mainstream. Sales professionals now use computers, cell phones, PDAs, e-mail, and the Internet to do their work. At the same time, laws have changed about using the telephone to sell, making it more challenging to effectively use the telephone.

In spite of all of the change, one thing has remained constant: the fact that the telephone is still the best and most direct way to generate new business.

Selling is a relationship business. In order to sell something, you need to get to know your customers. You need to understand their needs. How are you going to do this without developing a personal relationship?

Whether you sell exclusively by telephone or use the phone to get a face-to-face appointment, prospecting starts the relationship-building process.

Recently, our company had the honor of training one of the world's largest and most successful corporations. Because it had such a strong reputation, customers had always sought them out. It had never really been proactive in terms of new business development. Its industry was in an economic downturn of sorts, and it needed to start looking for business. We were asked to train its global sales organization in the prospecting and new-business-development process, the exact process outlined in this book. When we started the project, we found that most of the company's sellers either did no proactive new-business development or relied heavily on e-mail for their new-business development efforts. Their current approach was not yielding the type of results required by the corporation or by Wall Street.

The company's sales force was very skeptical about prospecting. After all, it was a mature sales organization, and it considered prospecting more appropriate for newer sellers. They worked for a technology company and felt that e-mail was the best way to generate new business.

With the full support of top management, we were able to convince the sales organization to attend the seminars and to start prospecting. Within a few months it was closing more sales than it had thought possible.

Here was one of the most mature and sophisticated sales organizations in the world. Its company was world renowned, and so was its selling prowess. The sellers were extremely adept at using technology. But they had gone off track, and it took good old-fashioned prospecting and your basic telephone to get this behemoth back on track. To make a long story short, telephone prospecting worked. And it worked extremely well.

Yes, prospecting by phone still works. It works better with the use of technology and the Internet, and it works in spite of the new telecommunications laws. So, let's get ready to pick up the phone and boost our income.

Before we get any further into the book, it's important for you to know that I will be selling right up until my last breath. In fact, when I leave this worldly plane, I fully expect to go to heaven. For me, heaven will be a small room with a telephone and a never-ending list of prospects. While this may sound a bit cynical, you cannot succeed at what you do not love. I am going to work very hard at making sure you love to prospect.

Loving Sales

Before we begin, I would like to tell you a little bit more about me. My professional selling career began during graduate school. I'd just completed my first year in the master of business administration program at the William E. Simon Graduate School of Business Administration at the University of Rochester. I was majoring in public accounting and finance. I was searching for a summer job (the university called it an "internship") and wound up with a company that sells wire rope.

For those of you who do not know, wire rope is the cable that holds up bridges. It is also used to raise and lower elevators. It is not the most exciting product in the world, and much, if not all, sales activity takes place over the phone. If you are thinking that I was not particularly suited for the job, you are right. I had no formal or informal experience in sales. However, this was the only job opportunity that I had. I took it!

Little did I know what I was in for. I was so petrified that I went the entire summer without making one sale. I did everything I could to avoid picking up the phone, and I didn't do any prospecting. However, I did learn from the experience. Today, I am an entrepreneur. I have built two successful businesses of my own and attribute much of my success to my cold-calling prowess. I am so confident in my abilities that I honestly believe I could get an appointment with the president of the United States, should I so desire.

However, my success is no accident. Over the years, through trial and error, experience and study, I have developed a prospecting and business-development system that works! This system is outlined in this book. The system includes a number of strategies that will increase your probability of success in the sales cycle.

My recommendations are based on actual experience. I sell. Day in and day out, I sell. Since the mid-1980s, I have done nothing but sell, and I will continue to sell as long as physically possible. Accordingly, these recommendations are not textbook recommendations. Every day, I meet with customers and prospects, and the experiences that I have are the same exact ones that you have or will have. I feel the same pressures, fear the same rejections, and have all of the same concerns that you do. I know my recommendations work!

My experience with prospecting began when I started my first business, a computer training company, in 1983. I had just left a comfortable job with Price Waterhouse, the public accounting giant. When

I opened the business, the company had no customers and the company had no sales.

My first reaction, being the good accountant I was, was to advertise. I placed a nice ad in the *New York Times* and waited for the phone to ring. However, a funny thing happened. The phone didn't ring! When you think about pressure, think about this. I had left a cushy job at Price Waterhouse and started my own business. I had borrowed $3,000 from my father and didn't have a large cushion to work with. Things were starting out on the wrong foot.

This is where cold-call prospecting comes in. Business development is a proactive process. You cannot sit and wait for things to happen. You must go out and make them happen. If you sit and wait for things to happen, you will only expedite your own failure.

I got on the phone and out in the street. I hustled and built a thriving business. Unfortunately, the recession of the early 1990s burst our bubble. I had built a sales organization for our computer training business by then and had stopped prospecting myself. After all, prospecting was not a dignified thing for the president of a successful company to do. My role in the company had evolved to that of visionary leader.

I had heard a speech about the recession. The speaker's main point was that you need not participate in the recession if you don't want to. Lacking in the speech, however, was the formula for success. Naively, I delivered my version of the speech to our sales organization. I declared that while the rest of the country would suffer through this economic downturn, we would not! The recession was just starting to impact the economy and our company, but we were in control of our own destiny. While my intentions were certainly honorable, the speech didn't work. Our sales were flat in a potentially high-growth industry. I started to look for ways to increase our sales, and the telephone was an obvious choice.

Toward the end of 1991, we began to sit down and hit the phones. At first, nothing seemed to happen, and we doubted ourselves. However, we persisted, and 1992 was our best growth year ever; we experienced a 62 percent year-over-year growth rate. We attributed our success to a heavy focus on business development—in other words, cold-call prospecting.

I have cold called to sell wire rope, to start two businesses, and to warm up a recession. However, possibly my best prospecting experience came when we decided to franchise our business. Ours was a conversion program, which means that you must already be in our business to qualify as a franchise prospect. We started the franchise program under a new corporate identity, and I was responsible for franchise business development. I had to go to the public library, get the yellow pages for a city that we wished to visit, and start calling to set up appointments.

I would almost like to say that you have not really cold called until you have called out of the yellow pages. While this may not be the single worst list in the world, it certainly ranks quite high. Yet, by employing the strategies outlined in this book, I was able to call into an unfamiliar city, selling an unknown and untested concept, to people I had never met before.

The end result was that I regularly set up six appointments a day, starting at 8:00 A.M. and ending at 6:00 P.M., one appointment every two hours. It was a long day, but it worked. Ultimately, our franchise system became the second largest in the United States in terms of both sales and locations.

This book will teach you what cold-call prospecting really is and why it is a key element in your selling success formula. You will also learn strategies to overcome the fear of rejection, perhaps the greatest challenge you will face in your journey to selling success. Our goal is to make you "rejection-proof."

This book outlines a formula called "Smart Prospecting," a proven method used to establish priorities in the prospecting and sales process. You will be presented with the "10 Commandments of Prospecting," a strategy that will enhance your probability of success in the sales cycle.

We will dissect a cold call and teach you an effective method for developing your own cold-calling script, including not only how to handle your initial conversation but also how to overcome objections and set up subsequent calls to the prospect. Finally, you will be presented with additional strategies that will help you improve the likelihood of a positive outcome in the sales cycle, including a "Cold-Calling Tool Kit" and a "Reporting and Tracking Tool Kit." We will close by revealing Prospecting's Great Secret!

Let's move on, learn, and most important, have fun.

Acknowledgments

To Christina Parisi, who really believed in me with a long-term book contract.

To Jacquie Flynn, for her excellent developmental efforts on the first edition.

To Mike Sivilli, for his excellent management skills.

To Jerilyn Famighetti, for her excellent copy editing.

To Jeremiah Birnbaum, for his great proofreading work.

To Marj Lazzara and Barbara Haley, for their great help back at the REDHOTSALES™ Ranch.

To Lynn Spiess, for all of her "special" help, support, and encouragement.

RED-HOT
COLD CALL
SELLING

Second Edition

CHAPTER I

Prospecting
An Essential Element to Your Selling Success

Not too long ago, our company had the honor of working with one of the largest banks in the world. We were working with their mortgage business here in the United States. Their business has enjoyed a significant boom since the turn of the century as interest rates declined to historic lows.

The company was often reaching its annual sales goals by April or May. And this was done in the absence of a proactive sales effort. This is not to degrade the sales organization in any way. The company had a great team. It's just that inbound demand for its products was so high that the loan officers had no time for a real proactive sales effort. Many of the loan consultants could be found at their desks at 11:00 P.M., still processing inbound loan applications.

Management of the company was concerned. There were a number of loan officers in the company who had never worked in other than a declining interest rate environment. What would happen when rates started to rise? Would the younger loan consultants even know how to sell in this type of an environment?

So, the bank brought us in to help it develop and implement a proactive new-business development process. This was its strategy to respond to a rising interest rate environment that was inevitable. Even though the bank brought us in to help, managers wanted to under-stand exactly how our programs and processes would help them face their dilemma. In fact, when you are in the training business, you always get asked about the results your programs will generate. Every-one knows that training is good for individuals, but its impact is often not apparent unless their progress is tracked.

Our client was no different. Bank managers wanted to know what results our programs would generate. After all, we were going to train their entire mortgage sales organization here in the United States. This would be a risky, costly, and time-consuming exercise for them. They have every right to ask this question. And it is incumbent upon us to have a valid answer.

The answer to this question is, of course, to track the progress of the sales organization. We are going to provide you with the methodol-ogy we used to do this later in the book so that you can track your own results; if you are a sales manager, vice president of sales, or business owner, you can track the results of your team.

However, at this point, it is sufficient to know that we were simply going to track the progress of the people in the program.

If you were to consider the prospecting process, it might have the following steps:

1. Pick up the phone and dial the number you are trying to call.

2. Speak to the person you intended to speak with.

3. Get a face-to-face selling appointment; or, if you are in tele-sales, enter the telephone discovery or needs assessment proc-ess, which is your equivalent of the face-to-face sales call.

4. Develop a proposal. Here, a proposal is simply a solution that you offer to customers that they can purchase. It doesn't have to be lengthy and written. It can be brief and even verbal. The key concept for you to understand is that, on the basis of your proposal, long or short, written or verbal, the customer or pros-pect has something she can buy.

5. Win or close a sale on the basis of your proposal from step 4.

The first action item that we asked the sellers to complete, after doing their market intelligence research (which we are going to talk about extensively later in this book in Chapter 5, on Smart Prospecting), is to actually pick up the phone five times a day and dial the phone so that it rings. That's it.

We asked them to pick up the phone, press the appropriate buttons, and make the phone ring. It didn't even matter if someone at the other end picked up the phone. The goal was is simply to make the phone ring.

Before we talk more about what we saw, I want to share an interesting insight with you. When we started working with this company, most of its sales force was not doing any prospecting. Inbound demand for the company's products was so significant that the sales force had no time to focus on new-business development. However, things were going to change!

I am used to making many calls a day when I prospect. Sometimes, when I tell executive management teams what my expectations are, they think I am out of my mind.

If you are essentially doing no prospecting, suddenly switching to doing a lot of prospecting can be overwhelming. An easy-to-understand analogy is to imagine you have never run in the past and you are going to take up running to get yourself in shape. Depending on your current physical condition, you may start out with a quarter mile or maybe just a little bit more.

The level of prospecting that I was recommending to the bank seemed like an unattainable goal. So, we negotiated with executive management and came up with the idea of making five calls per day. Five calls a day is a very attainable goal. In addition, if one sales person makes five calls a day, he makes 25 calls a week. Assuming there are 50 workweeks in a year, just to make the math easy for all of us to see and understand, the same sales professional makes 1,250 incremental prospecting or new-business calls per year.

Let me ask you a simple question. Let's say that you made 1,250 incremental new-business development calls this year. Do you think you would sell more this year than last? Of course you would. In fact, you would sell a lot more than you did last year.

Prospecting is a highly leveragable way to spend your time as a sales professional. For a small increment in effort (five calls a day), you can have a major impact on your business over the course of a year (1,250 incremental calls per year).

There are two other things you can learn from this.

First, if you can't make five calls a day, make four calls a day. And, if you can't make four, make three. If you can't make three, make two; and if you can't make two, make one incremental prospecting or new-business development call a day.

Never go down to zero. That is simply unacceptable.

If you make the one incremental call per day, that amounts to five calls per week and 250 calls per year. Even that will have a major impact on your business.

The second thing is also very simple.

Once you figure out that you can make one call per day, try to make two calls per day. The incremental effort on your part is minimal, and the impact on your business is significant.

When you make the incremental one call, whom are you helping? You are helping yourself. The only possible outcome of making more calls is that you will make more money. I'm sure that is one of the reasons that you entered sales. In sales, there is really no limit to your success.

When we implemented this system at the bank, the first thing that I noticed was that the sales force started to make some calls—not as many as I would have liked, but they did get the process started. Just by calling, they were able to speak with decision makers, the next step in the prospecting process. These were the primary results we observed in the first month of the implementation—dials and completed calls. Next came month two, and the process continued. More calls were made, and more calls were completed; however, the important difference between month one and month two was that the sales organization was now going on to many face-to-face meetings, the third step in the prospecting process.

Our client was incredibly pleased with the results, and also surprised. One of the bank's primary objectives in implementing the program was to increase customer face time. In month two of the implementation, we were already doing that.

It is important to note that while our client was surprised, I was not. Prospecting has a very predictable result. It's like anything else. If you put more effort into the process, you achieve a greater result. Any of us who has ever worked out to get into shape, dieted to lose weight, or budgeted to save money for the future knows what I am talking about.

As you work out, you continue to improve your conditioning. As you diet, you continue to lose weight, and as you save for your future, your money grows and grows. In fact, it was Albert Einstein who said that his greatest discovery was the compounding of interest. What he learned was that as you save money, your savings grow as a result of the process. However, what Einstein was talking about was that the saving process actually takes on a life of its own through the compounding of interest. Your money actually starts to work for you.

Believe it or not, prospecting is no different. As you continue to prospect, the process takes on a life of its own. Your prospects start to recognize you and your company, they start to admire your persistence, and you develop recognition in the market that you could not achieve otherwise. In fact, the more you prospect, the easier it gets.

So, in month two, the meetings started to happen. In month three, we saw a lot of new proposals being issued, and by month four, the sales started to happen. There was no magic here. All that we observed was the prospecting process in action.

I like to say that selling success is the only possible outcome of the prospecting process. Be aware, however, that your success will never be immediate. As you can see from the case study that I am sharing with you, it took several months for the process to start. This is what we call the sales cycle. Unfortunately, you can't make up your mind to sell today and start to generate significant revenue today. It takes time, and this time, again, is called the sales cycle. As you can see from the example, sales started to happen in a significant and predictable way in month four. An average sales cycle is usually four to six months long. It can be shorter if the dollar value of the sale is lower, and it can be longer if the dollar value of the sale is extremely significant.

There is one other interesting observation that I would like to make. As you can see from the sales cycle and the example that we just reviewed, it takes four to six months, on average, for the benefits of prospecting to start to impact your business. What I would like to do now is discuss what happens when you forget the basics and stop prospecting.

When you stop prospecting, you will still have a pipeline of prospects from your old prospecting efforts. However, the pipeline will get smaller and smaller because you are not filling the pipeline with new prospects (since you stopped prospecting). Eventually, the pipeline will dry up, and you will have only your current opportunities to work one. This is the single worst place a sales professional can be—working only on current opportunities.

Eventually, your current opportunities will all come to closure as you either win or lose the sale. And what happens next? You will be left with very little to do. You will have few or no current opportunities to work on, and you will have no new opportunities because you ceased prospecting many months ago. So, you are going to be faced with a significant revenue challenge. You will have no revenue, and you will have nowhere to go to start immediately generating revenue. This tells you that prospecting *must* be part of your daily activities, *no matter what.*

You can always justify not prospecting in your mind. You will probably say to yourself and your manager that you are too busy working on your current opportunities. But when you say this, it is as if you are saying that you are going to the gym to exercise and then stopping at the ice cream parlor, instead. You are engaging in activities that will not lead you to your long-term goals. Sure, the ice cream tastes good now, and, sure, life is better when you don't prospect (at least it's easier), but over the long run, you will be a lot better off if you exercise and if you prospect than if you kid yourself with false ideas.

There is one other interesting point here.

When you are in the position of having no current opportunities to work on and no future opportunities to work on, you always come up with the same idea—*prospecting!* The only problem is that you should have thought about prospecting months before you got into this position. It's too late to start now. It's clearly better than nothing, but you can see now that your revenue stream is about four to six months over the horizon.

Prospecting and business development are possibly the most crucial elements in your selling success formula. Most salespeople realize this. However, most salespeople do not enjoy prospecting and try to minimize the time spent in this area.

As you will see, if you are not successful at prospecting, it's unlikely you'll be a successful salesperson, but if you are, you will undoubtedly be successful in one of the most challenging and rewarding careers this country has to offer. Let's see why.

Steps in the Sales Cycle

A sample sale cycle might have the following steps:

1. Planning

2. Prospecting

3. Meeting

4. Recommending

5. Closing

6. Servicing

Although you will clearly be more effective if you plan your sales activities, planning is not a prerequisite to prospecting. You can always take a copy of the local yellow pages (as I have done), begin with the As, and continue on until you reach the end of your selling career. This strategy will not maximize the return on the time you invest in the sales process, but it will allow you to move forward.

Prospecting, on the other hand, is clearly a prerequisite to the remainder of the selling cycle. If you are not effective at prospecting or business development, you will never have the opportunity to be effective at any remaining element in the sales process. You will never be able to meet prospects, recommend appropriate solutions for their needs, close sales, and provide exceptional postsale customer service.

Given this fact, you could easily conclude that if you are not effective at prospecting, you will not be effective at selling. While the same could be said of any remaining step in the sales cycle, you will clearly reach a premature dead end because of your lack of effectiveness in the prospecting area.

This book is devoted to the fine art of prospecting and business development. Together, we are going travel a path that will completely reengineer your outlook toward business development. As we travel on this journey, one of my goals is to present a few new ideas that will enhance your probability of success in the sales cycle.

Your Path to Success

Enhancing your probability of success in the sales cycle is a crucial point. Sales is a highly competitive business. It should come as no surprise that if you are not calling on your customers and prospects, someone else will be. Accordingly, it is critical that you obtain every possible edge. During my studies of sales and motivation, I have learned that the differences between the winners and losers, the top performers and the average performers, are not large. Rather, the top performers in a given field are doing things just slightly better than the others in their profession. In sales, for example, the top producers might make that one extra call or attend that one extra sales meeting. Although the difference in performance is not substantial, the difference in income for the top performers can be significant.

Consider Jack Nicklaus, perhaps the greatest golfer of all time. During one year in the 1960s, at or near the peak of his skills, Nicklaus earned approximately $400,000 on the PGA tour. There was another golfer on the PGA tour that year, as well. His name was Bob Charles. As a professional, Bob Charles was not as successful as Jack Nicklaus. During that same year, Bob Charles earned approximately $40,000 on the PGA tour; the difference in earnings between Bob Charles and Jack Nicklaus was approximately tenfold (excluding income from endorsements and other revenue-generating activities). It might surprise you to learn that the difference in their respective per-round stroke averages was less than half a stroke. Imagine that! The difference between the greatest golfer of all time and a very good golfer was less than one-half stroke per round.

This phenomenon takes on even more significance in the world of professional selling. After all, Bob Charles still got paid even if he came in second, third, or tenth. Suppose you are competing with another company for a sale. You submit your proposal and feel that you have done the very best you can. Further, you feel that this is one of the very best jobs you have ever done. You call up the prospect to find out his decision. He tells you that you wrote an excellent proposal and did a really great job of understanding his needs. Then he tells you that had it not been for this other company, you would have won the work. Your proposal was second best.

How much revenue does your company earn when you come in second? How much commission do you earn when your company comes in second? The answer to both questions is obvious, which is why it is absolutely crucial that you make every effort to give yourself that competitive edge. The recommendations in this book are designed to do just that—to give you that competitive edge, or to enhance your probability of success in the sales cycle.

Let me give you a personal story.

When I started my second company, a sales training company, I again found myself in the position of having no customers and no sales. This was the second time in my life that I was in this position. The first, of course, was when I started my first company, the computer training company.

This time, fortunately, I was older and wiser. My approach to the market was much more sophisticated this time. When I started the sales training company, I actually targeted specific high-potential accounts. You may think that this is trivial issue, but it is not.

Most salespeople, including myself, follow the path of least resistance. We do what is easiest, not what is best. One way this manifests itself in sales behavior is to call potential clients, but not the very best prospects in the market.

We are going to talk more about this when we get to Chapter 5, the "Smart Prospecting" section of the book, but you should be able to understand, at this point in the book, that one way to prioritize prospects is by buying potential. And, one way to accomplish this is to measure buying potential by the size of the company in terms of its gross sales.

What I am saying here is that the larger companies in the market might be one place to start your prospecting efforts. Again, we are going to discuss this in great depth when we discuss Smart Prospecting. For now, to go back to my example, I actually followed my own advice.

I went to Hoovers Online, a resource that I use to provide a foundation to my prospecting efforts. I am going to discuss how you can use Hoovers later in the book. I live in New York State, so I downloaded a list of the largest companies in New York State.

At the top of the list was IBM. It had more than 300,000 employees at the time, and I assumed that they would need lots of sales training. So, I started to call. I started in 1997 and didn't get my first appointment until 2000. And, it is important for you to know that I had developed a number of contacts to call over the three years.

In any event, I made many calls each year, without success. Then, one day, I had a conversation with an executive and got my first face-to-face meeting. The meeting resulted in my first small sale at IBM in 2001. Today, IBM is our largest client.

If you remember, I was pointing out that the difference between winning and losing in sales is not a large difference. Rather, it is a small difference on the margin.

What would have happened if I had given up and not made that last call? I would not have gotten that crucial first small sale, and today IBM would not be our largest account. What's worse is that some other salesperson might have gotten that first sale instead of me.

If I had opted not to make that last reward call, someone else would have, and this story (and the money that went along with it) would belong to someone else.

My second objective in writing this book is to remind you of certain things that you may have already learned and since forgotten. In fact, I often say that I have forgotten more about professional selling than I remember. In order to keep sharp, I listen to a new audiocas-

sette program each week and read a new book each month. The benefits are astounding!

Let me tell you another illustrative story.

I was riding to a Fortune 200 account with one of our account
managers. When we arrived, the prospect told us there was no way we
would ever do business with his company. The company was happy
with its present suppliers.

In the car, however, we had been listening to a Brian Tracy audio
program on professional selling. On the tape, he talked about the instant-reverse close. The instant-reverse close is designed to ask a question that will completely turn around an apparently dead-end
objection. I wasn't sure that either of us was even listening to the
program, but the message must have gotten through to our subcon-
scious minds.

When faced with the ultimate rejection, the account manager I
was with simply asked the prospect what he would do if he were in
our shoes and had just heard his response (the instant reverse). He
directed us to his manager, the true decision maker in the company.
Following through on the instant-reverse close, we wound up doing
business with the company.

The point is, we can all learn. I am counting on you to keep an
open mind and, more important, to have fun as you learn—my third
objective for this book.

You see, I love professional selling. In fact, I cannot think of anything I'd rather be doing as far as my career is concerned. It is an
exciting job with ample opportunity for financial rewards. Further,
selling is extremely challenging. I liken it to a nice round of golf in
that you are never presented with the same shot twice, no matter how
many times you play the same course. Selling, like golf, presents a
unique opportunity each time you meet a prospect or customer.

CHAPTER 2

What Is Prospecting?

I am a strong proponent of the idea that in order to be successful at an occupation, you must enjoy what you do. At a minimum, you spend roughly one-third of your adult life at work. How can you possibly be successful if you do not enjoy what you do?

My experience has been that most salespeople love the sales but could live without the prospecting. I and others have traced the lack of enthusiasm back to a fear of rejection. This fear can paralyze almost anyone in any profession or endeavor and often leads to a failure to achieve selling success.

The trick is to alter your perceptions of prospecting and rejection. We could offer a number of sophisticated psychological techniques to help you. I prefer to keep it simple and suggest several fun strategies. You can pick the one that works best for you.

Is the Glass Half-Full or Half-Empty?

Prospecting, like anything else, can be viewed positively or negatively. In other words, is the glass half-full or is it half-empty? If you believe that the glass is half-empty and choose to focus on the rejection involved in prospecting, then it's very easy to see why you might not find prospecting an enjoyable part of your job.

On the other hand, there are many positive elements about prospecting. Viewing the glass as half-full will allow you to see prospecting from a completely different, and positive, perspective. Most important, you will be taking your first steps toward becoming "rejection-proof." Figure 2-1 offers a definition of prospecting that allows us to begin viewing the glass as half-full.

Figure 2-1 tells us that prospecting is the conversion of a stack of leads into a stack of money through the effective use of the telephone.

While you may believe that this definition is a bit farfetched, it is not. As a sales professional, I firmly believe that your most valuable financial asset, including your home, your savings accounts, and your investments, is your database and contact list.

Consider the facts.

When I started my second company, the Sales & Performance Group, now a global sales and marketing training company, I was working from a small home office. The entire company was me, sitting in a room, with a desk, a chair, a telephone, and a computer.

If this scene seems familiar, it should. If you return to the preface of the book, you will see that this is my definition of heaven. The only thing that has changed over the years that have elapsed since I first wrote the book is that heaven, for me, now includes a computer.

In any event, let's get back to the story. When I started the company, I had only a few contacts in my contact list. These were people that I knew from my computer training company, the one that I had built up and sold. There were a few people from my prior organization who might be interested to learn about what I was doing after I sold the company. After all, sales training, which is what I do now, is not a terribly far cry from computer training, the business I had sold.

FIGURE 2-1 Prospecting defined.

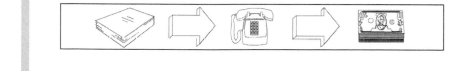

The point is that at the time I started my sales training company, I had very few contacts. Now our company is a global sales and marketing training organizations with locations all over the world.

My personal database has grown from only a few names to a corporate database with tens of thousands of contacts around the world. If you were to chart the growth of the database simply in terms of number of contacts in relation to the revenue growth of the company, you would see that the two are directly related. There is a strong correlation between the number of people that you know and your success in sales.

Hence, cold-call prospecting is the conversion of a stack of leads into a stack of money through the effective use of the telephone.

Keeping Track of Contacts

There is also one other interesting (and perhaps crucial) point here. Because your database or contact list is the source of your future income, it ought to be treated like gold. Your database is your most valuable asset.

For now, let's take the value of your database at face value.

You know that gold, the metal, is made up of smaller components, known as atoms. And the atoms, too, are made of smaller parts.

The same is true of your database. Your database is your pile of gold, but it is also made of smaller elements, the individual names in your list. The individual names on your list must be treated as a precious asset because it is to these individuals that you will actually sell at some point. It is the individuals who personally account for your future income.

Whether you work from a computer to manage your contact list, and I certainly hope that you do, or prefer some kind of manual system, you need to treat each individual contact with extreme care. This means that when you are working with a particular individual, you should study the information you can see about that person.

If I am working from my computer, I try to associate the contact name with a contact company. This is important for callbacks. I've seen many a salesperson stumble when receiving a callback from a prior prospecting call, only because the salesperson did not study the contact information when making the original call.

By associating the contact name with the company, you will be able to better remember the person's needs and integrate your thoughts into the early stages of your next call. An important point here is to keep up your database. People move around a lot, so you'll want to make sure you have the name of the new person in any position and also keep track of the person who is leaving. Knowing where a contact worked before is helpful, too.

In addition, I try to remember key elements of a conversation, such as the particular issue, product, or service that we were talking about. Again, I do this because I want to rapidly recall the context of our conversation if I happen to receive a callback from the contact that I did not anticipate.

I'm sure this seems like a lot of work, but it's really not. I do most of the studying when the phone is ringing and when I am getting transferred to an extension or voice mail. I try to make the most of my time. Computer programs have made this extremely easy.

If you are not using some form of computerized contact management system (e.g., some of the smaller, individual or small-business solutions like ACT! or Goldmine, or some intermediate CRM system for medium-size businesses such as Salesforce.com, or some enterprisewide system for large organizations, such as Seibel), you cannot claim to be a real business developer. Not using a computer program will hold you back.

I have more than 8,000 contacts in my database. I have years worth of notes, histories, interrelationships within the data, and a lot of future follow-up information. This amount of data requires a computer program to process it.

Business development is a sophisticated, comprehensive, time-sensitive process. Cell phones, PDAs, manual systems, and other limited data management devices can help, but they don't replace a CRM program. In fact, that is the first way I assess someone's business-development prowess. If you can't keep track of all this information, you cannot be a black-belt business developer. You need a large, com-

prehensive contact list to rank among the best, and you need a computerized system to manage your comprehensive data list.

Your Most Valuable Asset

Your contact list is your most valuable asset, even more valuable than
your house. Let's see why.

Let us assume that you are a commissioned salesperson and that
you make $50,000 per year. Let us also assume that you are 30 years
old and that you will work until you are 60. Finally, let us assume that
you will never earn any more or less than $50,000 per year and that
you are compensated solely on the basis of commission.

Using these assumptions, your database will generate an income
stream for you of $3 million over your work life expectancy. That's not
too bad. I suppose that a $100,000 house that you purchase could
perform in a similar way over the 30 years, but I think you can see
what a valuable asset your contact list is. It is something that should
be treated with extreme care.

Viewing prospecting in this manner allows us to focus on the positive outcome of the process (sales) and to leave the negative element
(rejection) completely out of our definition. If you take this definition
to its logical extreme, it would be hard to think of a better way to earn
a living! Imagine another job that allows you to get paid for simply
dialing the telephone.

Of course, it's not quite *that* easy. After all, our first definition did
have the word *effective* as one of its key elements. Being effective is
clearly a crucial element to your overall success and is a topic we are
going to explore in depth when we discuss Smart Prospecting. At this
point, however, I would like to work with our basic premise a little
longer.

There is an old story about a man who is using a sledgehammer
to try to break a large rock. He hits the rock once, and nothing happens. He hits it again, and nothing happens. He continues, hitting the
rock a hundred times without any results. Finally, on the next try, the
rock shatters and breaks into many small pieces.

In order to understand this story, one must ask whether the rock broke solely because of the final blow or because of the cumulative effect of all blows. If you are like me, you understand that the rock broke because of the cumulative effect. This understanding allows us to further develop our definition of prospecting.

The Sun Does Rise in the East and Set in the West

In Chapter 13, we are going to spend a good deal of time discussing how to track your prospecting efforts. Without getting into too much detail at this point, I'd like you to consider the segment of a sample weekly sales report in Figure 2-2. Please note that the information provided in the report is for illustration purposes only.

Here, dials are simply the number of times you pick up the phone and press the number indicated on your lead sheet. Completed calls are the number of times that you actually reach the person you intended to when you initiated the call. This does not include voice mail or the person's assistant. The remainder of the definitions—appointments, proposals, sales, and sales $—should be self-explanatory.

The crucial point here is that there is a clear and distinct relationship between the number of times that you dial the phone and the sales volume that you ultimately generate for your company. When we cover reporting and tracking in more detail, we are going to strongly urge that you consider keeping detailed records of your prospecting activities. This will help you to better understand the relationship between dialing the phone and sales volume. Suffice it to say that if

FIGURE 2-2 Information from a weekly sales report.

Dials	Completed Calls	Appointments	Proposals	Sales	Sales $
100	50	13	13	5	$20,000

you keep accurate records, you will soon learn that your relationship between sales volume and dials of the telephone can be as predictable as the sun rising in the East and setting in the West, irrespective of your prospecting acumen. The tools and ideas presented in this book will simply improve your relationships (between sales volume and dials of the telephone) or, as we said in the first chapter, enhance your probability of success in the sales cycle.

What's in It for Me?

I'd like to continue with the example and include one more important point. Please consider the relationship presented in Figure 2-3.

What you should notice is that the relationship we established earlier, between sales volume and dials of the telephone, actually extends beyond that point to a salesperson's commission check—that is, the size of one's commission check is directly related to the number of times one dials the telephone.

Putting a slightly different twist on this observation, one could argue that a salesperson earns money each and every time she dials the telephone, irrespective of the outcome of the call. In this example, the salesperson earns $10 each time she dials the phone. This under-

FIGURE 2-3 The commission-dialing connection.

Dials	Completed Calls	Appointments	Proposals	Sales	Sales $
100	50	13	13	5	$20,000

Sales	$20,000
Dials	100
Sales/dial	$200
Commission rate	5.00%
Commission/dial	$10

standing lies in the fact that one cannot tell in advance which calls will be the ones that yield the sales. As with the man's effort to break the rock, it is the cumulative effect of the prospecting efforts that leads to selling success, not the impact of any given call. This interpretation leads us to the second definition of prospecting as the opportunity to earn income each and every time one dials the telephone.

The chart in Figure 2-4 allows us to take our analysis one step further. What you should notice is that if you increase your level of prospecting activity, your sales volume and ultimately your income will increase as well. Hence, prospecting gives you the opportunity to set your level of income.

This definition of prospecting probably explains the decision of most of the people who enter the world of professional selling. As a salesperson, you have the opportunity to set your level of income. If you wish to increase your level of income, increase your prospecting activity. If (for some reason) you wish to decrease your level of income, decrease your prospecting activity. The results will be very predictable.

Next, consider the relationship between prospecting activity and income and how these relate to downturns in the business environment. When the economy enters an economic downturn, or recession, business activity doesn't cease; it simply slows down. The rate at which the economy slows is indicative of the depth of the recession. I heard a very clever speech about one's decision to participate in a recession. I thought the speech was so good that I even gave my own interpretation of the facts to our sales organization. What I learned, all too late, was that while the message was right on target, it lacked a specific and

FIGURE 2-4 More sales report information.

Dials	Completed Calls	Appointments	Proposals	Sales	Sales $
100	50	13	13	5	$20,000
200	100	25	25	10	$40,000
400	200	50	50	20	$80,000

definite course of action for follow-up. Through trial and error, and after many aggravating days, I finally found the secret. Here it is.

A recession, to a salesperson, simply means that the relationships defined in this chapter are slightly altered. During a recession, you have to make more calls to yield the same results. But you can still obtain those results if you wish. Further, with a small increase in effort, you may even be able to exceed prior performance levels. Not only does prospecting give you the opportunity to set your level of income, but it also gives you the opportunity to determine the extent to which you wish to participate in an economic downturn.

I have heard many stories about salespeople succeeding in a recession far beyond what they had achieved prior to the downturn. Perhaps they understood the ideas outlined in the preceding paragraphs. Couple these ideas with the fact that many of their competitors may have lost their focus, or may have gone out of business, during the same recession and the results can be significant. After all, most salespeople probably give up during a recession. So while the total pie is smaller, your slice can be proportionately quite a bit larger.

The Law of Sowing and Reaping

I started my entrepreneurial career in the computer training business and have always tried to encourage people to use technology. I might have overstepped my boundaries in trying to impress on my mother, a sales veteran of many years, that automation should be part of her sales arsenal. She told me that salespeople had been selling long before there were computers. In fact, she taught me that references to professional selling actually can be found in the Bible. Let's see where.

The Bible makes reference to the Law of Sowing and Reaping. The Law of Sowing and Reaping tells us, "Whatever ye shall soweth, so shall ye reapeth." As you will soon see, the Law of Sowing and Reaping is a biblical paradigm for professional prospecting and professional selling. In fact, the Law of Sowing and Reaping is the foundation for the relationships I have outlined and lends further credence to the relationship among dials of the telephone, sales volume, and income.

Imagine you were a farmer and planted a crop of only one seed. What type of harvest could you expect down the road? You wouldn't expect to see much of a harvest at all. However, if you planted many seeds and properly cultivated those seeds, you would typically expect an abundant harvest at the end of the season. Selling, and in particular prospecting, is no different from farming. The seeds that you plant are your cold calls. Plant only one seed, or make only one cold call, and you cannot expect to have an abundant harvest at the end of your sales cycle. However, plant many seeds, or make many cold calls, and, like the farmer, you can expect an abundant harvest at the end of your sales cycle.

I am sure that all of us are too familiar with those desperate feelings that often accompany business development and sales. Why didn't they call me back? I have to get that appointment! I need to make this sale! These situations all result in the same uncomfortable, queasy feeling. Each time I get this feeling, I know that I haven't planted enough seeds. The Law of Sowing and Reaping, which tells us to be sure to plant enough seeds, can be the best remedy for this upset stomach.

Looking at this situation from another perspective can also be quite enlightening. Imagine that, as a farmer, you had an abundant harvest. How would you feel? Of course, you would be quite proud of your efforts. However, in light of your abundant harvest, would you think that every single seed you planted succeeded? Of course not. There will always be seeds that don't germinate. With an abundant harvest, you probably wouldn't even notice the seeds that didn't grow! That's right—the abundant harvest (your success) has completely overshadowed the fact that certain seeds didn't grow (your failures). If you are successful at prospecting, your successes will overshadow your failures, and you will soon learn that there is no better way to earn a living.

A Positive Outlook

Napoleon Hill, the author of *Think and Grow Rich,* once said that there are three sides to every story: my side, your side, and the correct side, which probably lies somewhere in between. There is great wisdom in these words. Some, including myself, would argue that prospecting is great fun. Others would argue that it is not. Prospecting can be fun if you give it a chance. Remember, prospecting not only gives you the opportunity to earn money each and every time you dial the telephone; it also gives you the opportunity to set your level of income. Prospecting is also quite challenging. What more could you want in a career?

Now that we have a positive outlook on the prospecting process, let's move on to the next chapter and learn why prospecting is an essential element in your business-development success formula.

CHAPTER 3

The Power of Prospecting

I'd like to reflect again on my first sales position: the summer intern-ship I had selling wire rope. Like all hardworking sales professionals, I would get to work by 8:00 A.M. My experience now tells me that the hour between 8:00 and 9:00 A.M. is one of the best times to prospect. This is particularly true now thanks to voice mail.

However, youth is wasted on the young, as the saying goes. My typical workday would start with an hour of coffee drinking, newspa-per reading, and talking with the other folks in the company. No calls were made.

I would then move on to one of professional selling's greatest ritu-als: "lead sorting." This practice involves taking your leads and sorting them so that they are in the best possible order to begin your day's work. It is not clear to me why we engage in this curious behavior, as lead sorting has no direct, measurable impact on success in the sales process. Yet, most salespeople, if not all of us, sort our leads into the best possible order prior to beginning prospecting for the day. My lead-sorting routine would always take an hour or two, from 9:00 to 11:00. The end result was that I made no calls during that time. By 11:00, I was faced with a grave dilemma.

I assumed that all of my prospects were preparing to go to lunch. Being polite, I did not want to interrupt their preparation process, so I made no calls between 11:00 and noon. I also assumed that my prospects were out to lunch between noon and 2:00. Not wanting to waste time on the phone if no one would be available, I made no calls during the lunch hours, either.

After lunch was also no time for prospecting. After all, your prospects had just returned from a fulfilling meal, and you did not want to give them indigestion. Being the consummate professional, I gave my prospects one hour to digest their lunch, from 2:00 to 3:00.

Finally, I closed out my day from 3:00 to 5:00. I must share with you that I was thoroughly exhausted at this point. I had come to work at 8:00, and I had done nothing but prospecting and business development (or so I thought) up until 3:00. I used the last hours of my day to wrap up, and I allowed my prospects to do the same. At 5:00 P.M., I left.

As you can see, the end result of this sophisticated process was that I made no calls.

The Law of Sowing and Reaping tells us that this places us in a very precarious position as sales professionals. If we do not make cold calls, we will have done little, if anything, to further our business development efforts.

Just Do It

Nike has a great motto that it has used for many years: "Just Do It!"

This is quite compelling for us as sales professionals.

Procrastination is a major issue for sales professionals. It can actually ruin our careers. There are actually two types of procrastination that I have learned about over the years.

The first type is the type that I exhibited in the anecdote I just related. There, I was unable to get started. I looked for every excuse not to prospect.

There is actually another type of procrastination that is just as bad. In fact, I think that this second type is far more common than the first. The second type of procrastination is procrastination between calls. Here, the seller endlessly researches the next call.

What did I say to the prospect the last time we spoke? What did he say to me? Let me go take a look at the customer's Web site. Let me search Google or Yahoo, for example, for current news on the customer.

I am not saying that research is not important. It is. In Chapter 5, I will show you exactly how to prepare for a call. For now, suffice it to say that research is good, but procrastination, or endless research, will hurt you quite a bit.

It is important for you to realize that as a professional salesperson, you have basically two crucial functions. Your first responsibility is to service your existing customers. Your second responsibility is toward business development.

This is what you are paid to do. When you are not providing superior customer service, you must devote your full attention and energy to business development and prospecting. They are crucial to your selling success.

As we all know, it is just too easy to avoid prospecting. I was very successful at avoiding my business development responsibilities in my first sales job, and it showed by virtue of the fact that I made no sales.

Since I wrote the first edition of this book, I have learned something that I believe you will find quite amazing. It is the secret of sales time management.

Sales Time Management

Since I have been in the sales business, I have learned that all sales professionals believe that they are working hard. I have also learned that all sales professional believe that they are investing adequately in the prospecting process and that all sales professionals (well, almost all sales professionals) fully believe that they are going to reach their sales goals right up until the final day.

Since all sales professionals fully believe that they are doing the right things in terms of their prospecting efforts, I have developed a specific formula to truly tell you whether you are or are not.

In order to understand my sales time management formula, you must first understand that there are three types of sales professionals: new, moderate, and top.

A new sales professional is one who is not generating much in the way of current revenue. There are two reasons for this. First, your sales could be limited because you are new to a company or new to an industry. It should come as no surprise that if you are just starting out, your sales will be quite limited.

Next, your sales could be limited because you are not doing very well. This, of course, could be the direct result of your prospecting efforts, or lack thereof.

In any event, it is not important to isolate the reason for your lack of production. For purposes of sales time management, a new sales professional is one who is not generating much in the way of current revenue.

Now, let's move on to the moderate sales professional. A moderate sales professional is one who is producing a "moderate" amount of revenue. If you were to consider a traditional bell curve, the moderate sales professional would be in the middle. There will be a select few who are doing better and an unfortunate few who are doing worse. Actually, most sales professionals worldwide fall into the moderate category. That is why the bell curve bulges in the middle.

Finally, there is the top sales professional, or the "top performer." This is what we all aspire to; however, only a few of us actually achieve this lofty goal. The top performer is that sales professional who is at the top of her class in terms of revenue production.

So, now we know that there are three types of sales professionals: new, moderate, and top. The next important step in our analysis is to understand that there are only three broad categories of things that we do as salespeople. They are, in order of importance, customer service, new-business-development, and nonselling activities. (I know that I said that there were only two activities earlier in this chapter, but if you go back and look, you will see that I said "crucial" activities. I strongly believe that customer service and new business development come far ahead of nonselling activities.)

In any event, let's take a look at the three activities of all sales professionals.

Whenever I deliver my seminars, I always get the response that 80 percent of a seller's time is taken up by nonselling activities. While

I know that this is an exaggeration and I am just trying to make a point, I have learned over the years that it is important to define what I mean by each of the three categories of activities.

Customer service is any activity that we engage in that relates to servicing an existing customer. Please note that my definition of a "customer" is any organization or individual, depending on whether you sell business-to-business or business-to-consumer, that you have done business with in the past 12 months.

So, if you did a million dollars' worth of business with a "customer" three years ago but have done no business with this customer over the past 12 months, my definition would consider this organization or individual to be a prospect.

Likewise, if you did a million dollars' worth of business with a "customer" 13 months ago, that customer would have just transitioned from true "customer" status to prospect status.

My definition of a customer is any organization or individual with which you have done business over the past twelve months and my definition of customer service is any activity that you engage in with an existing customer.

Examples of customer service could be traditional, such as solving a particular customer problem or concern, or nontraditional, such as holding a meeting to grow the customer relationship, writing a proposal to expand the customer relationship, or even prospecting to new areas within the company.

My definition of customer service is quite expansive and, to understand the points that I am about to make, it is important that you embrace this expanded definition. For purpose of clarity, "customer service" is *any* activity that you engage in with an existing customer, including traditional and nontraditional examples.

Now we can move on to the next definition, that of "new business development." New business development is *any* activity that you engage in to get new customers. Again, this definition includes traditional elements, such as cold calling, and it also includes nontraditional elements, such as writing proposals for noncustomers (or prospects) and holding meetings with noncustomers to gather information relevant to writing a proposal.

Just to recap, since the definitions are so crucial to the points I am going to make, since they are so frequently misunderstood in my seminars, and since they are so crucial to your success and mine, I am going to repeat them.

Customer service is *any*, and I mean *any*, activity that one engages in with existing customers. This can include traditional problem solving and it could include nontraditional elements of the definition, such as expanding the relationship from one segment of an organization to another.

New business development is *any*, and again I mean *any*, activity that one engages in to obtain new customers. This, too, can include traditional elements, such as cold calling, and nontraditional elements, such as research to obtain new customers.

Finally, we get to nonselling activities. My definition of a nonselling activity is any activity that does not and could not directly lead to revenue generation. Good examples of nonselling activities include completing an expense report, attending a weekly, monthly, or quarterly sales meeting, attending sales training, and attending annual or semiannual staff reviews. The important points to note here are twofold.

First, the definition suggests that the activity must not directly lead to revenue production. Sales training could lead to revenue production, but I would argue that it does not lead to revenue production directly as would a proposal or a cold call.

Second, nonselling activities are a residual. What I mean by residual is that it is clearly secondary in terms of importance with respect to both customer service and new business development as defined earlier, and it is residual in terms of time allocation. In other words, you should complete your nonselling activities *after* you complete your customer service and new-business-development activities, not before.

Okay, now we have the three activities of all professional salespeople: customer service, new business development, and nonselling activities. We also have the three categories of professional sales development: new, moderate, and top. So where do we go from here?

The first thing that is important to recognize is that nonselling activities are not as overwhelming as first thought. If you reflect on our earlier discussion, you should recall that most sales professionals feel that nonselling activities consume a majority of their day.

However, if you consider my definitions of customer service and new business development, you should realize that many of the items you may have originally thought were nonselling activities actually fall under the categories of customer service and new business development.

A classic example of this is account planning. Most sales professionals do not enjoy account planning, and most sales professionals consider account planning a nonselling activity. Actually, when you consider my definitions, you see that account planning would be considered either customer service or new business development, depending on whether the account plan is for a customer or a prospect.

The point that I am trying to make is that nonselling activities do not consume as much of your day as you might think. I believe that nonselling activities usually account for anywhere from 10 percent of your workday or workweek on the low end to as high as 25 percent on the high end.

The second point that I wish to make is that nonselling activities typically do not vary significantly from one category of sales professional, say, new, to another category of sales professional, say, moderate or top.

If you recall, I suggested that completing expense reports, attending meetings, and attending sales training events might all be considered nonselling activities. If you think about it, the first thing that you should see is that nonselling activities do not vary significantly from sales professional to sales professional, irrespective of your category of sales development.

Assuming that you were in the new category, it would take you eight hours to complete a one-day sales training event. If you are in the moderate or top category, it would take you the same eight hours to complete the program. Nonselling activities do not vary considerably across the three stages of sales development. This is important, because customer service and new business development do change quite a bit from category to category.

The second important thing to note about nonselling activities is that they are typically not optional. In other words, let's say that your manager calls a meeting. In all likelihood, the meeting is not optional and must be attended by everyone on your team. The point I am trying to make here is that your nonselling activities can be treated as a given as far as sales time management is concerned, and, your nonselling activities take up a fixed portion of your workday or workweek.

The great lesson here is as follows. Since your nonselling activities take up a fixed portion of your workday (they do not vary across the levels of sales development, and they are not optional), sales time management comes down to one question:

How does one allocate their time between customer service and new business development? This is everything you need to know about sales time management in one, simple question. The reason that it is such a profound question is that salespeople worldwide tend to overinvest in customer service and underinvest in new business development.

I'm sure your manager has come to you and urged you to do more prospecting. I'm equally sure that you likely responded to your manager in the following way: *"Would you prefer that I service my existing customers and close my current opportunities, or would you prefer that I do more prospecting?"* This, of course, is a rhetorical question and one that will not lead you to your full potential. I would urge you not to think this way, because the real answer to the question is that you need to do both.

Yes, you may be very busy and yes, you may be doing very well this quarter or this year, but consider the following. What is going to happen to you when all of your current opportunities are closed, by your either winning or losing the sale? If you have done no prospecting, the answer should bring chills to your spine.

If you are not backfilling your sales pipeline with new opportunities as your current opportunities mature to closure, you will be left, at some point, with nothing in your sales pipeline. And, as you and I both know, this is a terrible place to be as a sales professional.

I was once asked by a major corporation to train all of its sellers in sales negotiations. The problem the organization was experiencing was that as the end of the quarter drew near, and as salespeople had to close business to meet their sales goals for the quarter, they began to lower their price, with each passing day, in order to both win the business and reach their sales goals. What I learned as I began to work with the company was that the sellers did not have a sufficient pipeline to negotiate from a position of strength. As such, it was not negotiations training that they needed; it was prospecting training that they needed. I will go on record by saying that the single best sales strategy in the world, bar none, is having a full sales pipeline. To do that, you must prospect.

Have you ever experienced a period of strong sales, only to have it followed by a period of weak sales? Of course you have. We all have. The reason this occurs is that, during periods when we are busy, we neglect the prospecting and new-business-development process. In order to have strong and steady sales all or most of the time, you must habitually engage in the new-business-development process. There is no getting around this reality. It is one of the universal truths for us in the sales world.

Let's get back to our original point by assuming that our nonselling activities are both nonoptional and take up 25 percent of your workday or workweek. I used 25 percent because it is at the top end of the range of time one would typically devote to nonselling activities, given the definitions that I have provided to you. If you are spending more than 25 percent of your time in nonselling activities, you may want to consider sitting down with your manager and analyzing how you are spending your time. I am sure you can do better.

So, if you are spending 25 percent of your workweek in non-selling activities, you have 75 percent of your workweek to devote to other activities. We have learned that these other activities are either customer service or new business development. That is it.

Let us assume that you are in the new category of sales development. This means that you are producing very little in the way of current revenue. If one is producing very little in the way of current revenue, how much time do you think that person needs to spend in the customer service area? The answer is probably not very much. One could argue, if you are just starting out, that you may spend no time in the customer service area because you have no customers to service, but I am not going to be that severe. I am going to be very gracious and assume that you are spending 10 percent of your time in the customer service area.

If you are spending 10 percent of your time in customer service and 25 percent of your time in nonselling activities, this means that you are spending 65 percent of your time (or at least you should be) in the new-business-development area.

I know that most sales professionals do not work a 40-hour workweek, but let's say that you do just to keep our calculations simple. Sixty-five percent of a 40-hour workweek is 26 hours per week, or approximately five hours per day. This means that you should be spending five hours per day, or the better part of your workday, trying to get new customers. Why? The answer should be quite obvious. You should be spending the majority of your time trying to get new customers because you do not have many existing customers. Stated more starkly, you honestly don't have much else to do.

However, please keep in mind that to say that one must spend 65 percent of one's time in the new-business-development process is simply not enough. You could spend your time as I did at the wire rope company. I thought I was engaging in new business development, but all I was really doing was passing time.

In sales, there are only two activities that really count: prospecting, or trying to get new customers, and meeting with customers and prospects to close business. It is important to put the five hours per day discussed earlier into one of these two activities. Since the fundamental activity is making calls (because the calls precede the meeting), let's start out there.

How many calls do you think you can make in one hour?

I know from experience that you will take a conservative position of, say, five to ten calls per hour. That is okay, because prospecting is a highly leveragable activity. Remember that if you truly believe that you can only make one call in a day, that still adds up to five, incremental, new business calls per week, which is 250 calls per year.

The Power of Five Calls

So how many calls do you think you can make in an hour? Believe it or not, you can actually make 20 to 30 calls per hour, but I am not going to hold you to that. Let's stick with the lower boundary of five suggested earlier.

If you make five calls per hour, you will make 25 calls per day, since you will be in the new category, devoting five hours (or 65 percent) of your day to prospecting. Twenty-five calls per day amounts to 125 calls per week, or 6,250 per year.

On one hand, 6,250 calls are a lot! If you made this many incremental calls per year, they would surely have an impact on your business. On the other hand, 25 calls per day is not really too much to ask if you are in the new category. Remember, you really don't have that much else to do.

Here's what I think you ought to do at this point.

If you are in the new category, start with the assumption of five calls per hour and make them each and every hour. When you learn that you can actually make five calls an hour comfortably, think about raising the total to six. When you believe that you can comfortably make six calls per hour, raise your hourly production to seven per hour, and continue this process. Remember, you are not doing this because I am asking you to and you are not doing this because your manager is forcing you to. You are doing this because you want to be successful. The more calls you make, the more successful you will be. Why would you want to place an upper boundary on your success?

Now let's continue on with our sales time management discussion. If you are making 25 incremental, new-business-development calls per day, you will start to schedule some face-to-face or discovery meetings.

Please note that if you are in field sales, a face-to-face or discovery meeting is one where you visit with the customer to learn about his needs. If you are in telesales, a discovery meeting is held over the telephone, not face-to-face with the customer. The point is that for purposes of time management, the two types of meetings are identical. A discovery meeting is a discovery meeting, and you will see that when we get to the chapters on scripting (Chapters 7 and 8), your objective of the prospecting call will be the same, irrespective of whether you are in field sales or telesales. The objective of a prospecting sale is to get a discovery meeting, either face-to-face or over the telephone.

As you start to set up discovery meetings, the time you have available for prospecting calls will actually diminish. Let's see how this happens.

Let's say that you set up one discovery meeting. If you are in field sales, you need to allocate two hours for a discovery meeting, one hour for travel and one hour for discovery. If you are in telesales, you need to allocate one hour for a discovery meeting.

Going back to our original example, we had asked a new account manager to make allocate five hours per day, or 65 percent of her time, to new business development. The five hours amounted to 25 calls per day. If you are in field sales and you set up one discovery meeting, we said that you would need to allocate two hours for the meeting. This means that on that particular day, your new-business-development time allocation is two hours of new business development related to the meeting and three hours of new business development related to your calls. On this day, you would expect to have one meeting and make 15 calls.

If you think I am being hard on you, I suppose that I am. However, the purpose of this book is to make you as good as you can possibly be. Do you think a gold medal winner in the Olympics actually skimps on preparation? If you want to be the gold medal winner in your company or in your business, you cannot skimp on your work ethic, either.

I would even go so far as to say that the best of us will be making calls on our cell phones as we drive to and from the customer. Use a hands-free kit. Imagine what would happen to your sales over the course of the year if you made 20 or 25 calls on these days (instead of 15) and still attended your one meeting. Of course, this would again have a major impact on your results.

People ask me in my seminars if it is okay to make cold calls on your cell phone. In this day and age, I think it is actually expected that you will use your cell phone as a leveragable business tool to grow your sales. There is nothing wrong with a dropped call. Simply redial the number, apologize, and continue with your call.

Now you are making many calls per day and attending many meetings per week as you start out in the new category of sales development.

Over time, your meetings will convert to proposals and your proposals will convert to sales. Unless you give up and stop prospecting, which many of your colleagues and competitors will, this is the only possible outcome.

As your sales grow, you move from the new category to the moderate category. As you move from the new category to the moderate category, only one thing changes as far as sales time management is concerned. The time you must allocate to customer service will go up, because you now have a number of customers, and, as a result, the time you have to allocate to new business development must go down.

In the new category, we assumed that you allocated 25 percent to nonselling activities, 10 percent to customer service, and 65 percent to new business development. In the moderate category, we can assume that customer service now accounts for 50 percent of your workday, leaving 25 percent for new business development.

Twenty-five percent of a 40-hour workweek is 10 hours per week, or two hours per day. At a minimum, this should yield 10 calls or one meeting per day. It is very likely that you will do better, but I want you to believe that you can accomplish the metrics I am suggesting in this book.

Again, if you are making 10 calls per day, this amounts to 50 per week, or 2,500 per year. As an alternative, you could be attending one meeting per day, five per week or 250 per year. In all likelihood, you will be achieving a combination of the two, but in either event your sales will continue to grow if you stick with it.

Before I get to the top category, I want to share with you one of sales' great secrets. Did you ever wonder why a bell curve looks like a bell when you apply it to sales results? Stated another way, did you ever wonder why most sellers wind up as moderate and only a few sellers ever make it to the top category?

The answer is simple given what we have just discussed.

Most sellers understand that they must prospect when they are in the new category. This should be obvious, and there should not be much else to do. However, when sellers get to the moderate category, they forget or don't want to remember about the basics, prospecting. Most sellers get very lazy when they get to the moderate category and simply do not do what it takes to get to the top. I know you are not one of the lazy ones if you are reading my book, so let's continue.

If you put in the effort as a moderate producer, you will get to the top. Again, there is no other possible outcome. And, when you get to the top, only one thing changes. The amount of time one allocates to customer service again goes up and the amount of time one allocates to new business development must go down. A top performer may devote 25 percent of his time to nonselling activities (note that this did not change across all three levels of sales development), 70 percent of his time to customer service, and only 5 percent of his time to new business development.

Please note that it is crucial that your new-business-development time never reach zero. If it does over an extended period of time, you will slowly move from top performer to moderate performer again. And then you will be forced to increase your call production because you will have tasted success in the past.

While 5 percent of a workweek may seem like a trivial investment in the new-business-development process, you already know enough to know that what I just said is not true. Five percent of a 40-hour workweek is two hours per week, or slightly less than half an hour per day. You know enough to understand that you can make one, two, three, or possibly four calls during this time, and you know how rapidly the call totals add up over the course of the year.

Even if you are busy beyond all imagination, I urge you to consider making one new-business-development call a day. Once you stop, it's very hard to regain your momentum.

Proactively Prospecting

I understand that it is not easy to keep to this pace constantly. Since it is so difficult to motivate yourself to prospect, I'd like to explore several *compelling reasons to prospect.*

First, if you are going to rely on mail or e-mail to get the job done, most prospects will never feel the impact of your efforts. You will get much greater results from the call.

With respect to paper mail, when you send unsolicited information, one of six outcomes is possible:

1. The prospect never receives the information for a variety of reasons.

2. The prospect receives the information and throws it in the garbage.

3. The prospect receives the information, reads it, and throws it in the garbage.

4. The prospect receives the information, reads it, and passes it on to someone else.

5. The prospect receives the information, reads it, and saves it for a later date.

6. The prospect receives the information, reads it, and calls you.

Unfortunately, the least likely outcome is the last one. Most prospects do not respond to the information we send. Prospecting is our opportunity, as salespeople, to be *proactive* instead of reactive.

The same is true of e-mail. Much of what you send may be blocked by spam filters. If your e-mail does get through to the prospect, the next most likely outcome is the delete button.

I'm sure that many of you have read Stephen Covey's excellent book, *The Seven Habits of Highly Effective People.* Habit One is the Habit of Proactivity. Proactivity gives you control of your own destiny, a primary motivation to join the profession of selling in the first place. Prospecting is the most proactive sales activity that there is.

I prefer to send information (by e-mail most likely) to support a phone call, not to pave the way for one. The difference is subtle but will decrease the length of your sales cycle dramatically.

Second, most people rise to challenges, and prospecting is quite challenging. In telephone prospecting, you have two to three minutes to convince a complete stranger to spend some of her valuable time with you. As most of us have learned, this situation can be quite a challenge. However, as we all know, it is very rewarding when you get the appointment. The reason getting the appointment can be so rewarding is that prospecting is a microcosm of the sales process. How do you feel when you make a sale? You feel great! Why? Because you reached a goal. The goal of a prospecting call is to get an appointment. When you get an appointment, you have reached your goal and should feel elated. In fact, you should feel no less elated than when you make a sale. Why? Because you just made one! You sold someone on the concept of spending some of her valuable time with you.

Third, your prospecting success will breed additional prospecting success. My father always used to tell me to "strike while the iron is hot." Reflect for a moment on the elation you feel when you get that key appointment at a major account. You feel great! You're on top of the world! It has been said that selling is the transfer of enthusiasm about your product or service from you to the buyer, because if the buyer feels as strongly about your product or service as you do, a sale will occur. When you feel great, you are more likely to be successful in your next prospecting call. That's right. Immediately after making one key appointment, get right back on the phone and make some more. Your enthusiasm will be contagious, and your probability of success will soar. Strike while the iron is hot!

Next, prospecting prevents the selling peaks and valleys from which most salespeople seem to suffer. Some peaks and valleys can be attributed to the seasonality of a business, but most can be attributed to inconsistent prospecting efforts. In Chapter 2, we learned about the strong relationship between the number of times you dial the phone and your sales volume. A consistent diet of prospecting calls will yield a consistently successful sales career, just as a consistent diet of healthy food will lead to a long and healthy life.

Finally, and most important, prospecting is fun. Prospecting and selling are fun! After all, where else can you get paid to talk on the phone, meet people, and serve their needs? Selling is a great profession, and you should relish your opportunity to be one of its proud members.

CHAPTER 4

Becoming Rejection-Proof

In Chapter 3, I shared with you an in-depth account of my first experience with professional selling. I had a very sophisticated daily routine. I hate to admit it, but the entire routine was developed with one goal in mind: I did not want to make any cold calls. At the time, all I knew was that I was petrified. I didn't know why. Now I know that I suffered from a tremendous fear of rejection.

I suspect that if we all sold long enough, we would eventually overcome our fear of rejection. From my perspective, I'm not sure why we should wait 20 years or so for this to happen. I'd like to offer a strategy that can help you overcome your fear of rejection now: the "Selling Life-Cycle Paradigm."

The Selling Life-Cycle Paradigm: Educating Your Prospects

A paradigm is simply a way of looking at something. The Selling Life-Cycle Paradigm teaches you to view sales as a process and not as an event. The goal of the sales process according to the Selling Life-Cycle Paradigm is to educate your prospects and customers. In other words, if your prospects knew exactly what you knew about your product or service and felt exactly as you felt about your product or service, they would buy it.

More specifically, selling is the process of educating your prospects about the value your product or service will add to the profitability of their organization. If you can demonstrate that your product or service will yield a superior return on their investment, they will buy. If you cannot, then you must return the prospect to the sales pipeline and continue the education process at a later point in time.

Once you can demonstrate that your product or service will yield a superior return on investment, you will have a customer. Continue to demonstrate that your product or service will yield a superior return on investment, and you will have a customer for life. However, the onus is on you to demonstrate the value you bring to the table, which is why I believe that selling is a lifelong education process. If the prospect does not buy, you simply have to do a better job in the education area.

Continuing the Selling Process

One can never be rejected as long as the selling process continues. By being persistent, by continuing the education process, and by repositioning your prospect to an appropriate position in your sales pipeline after a temporary setback in the sales cycle, you have the ability to control the ultimate outcome of the sales process and the ability to control any emotions associated with an apparent rejection. In fact, given this perspective of selling, you see that it is impossible to lose a sale. The Selling Life-Cycle Paradigm is further explained in Figure 4-1.

Most salespeople realize they need sales today. Most also realize that they will need sales tomorrow. What few salespeople realize is that they will also need sales one year from today and one decade from today if they plan on remaining in the field of professional selling. By viewing sales as a process and not as an event, our "no's" today plant the seeds for "yeses" one year from today and 10 years from today. Following this thought process, a rejection should never be viewed as a no. Rather, a rejection should simply be viewed as information about a given prospect that allows you to both properly position that prospect in your sales pipeline and focus the direction of your education process. This concept is illustrated in Figure 4-2.

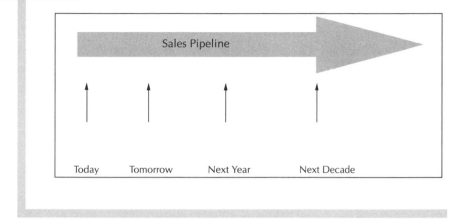

FIGURE 4-1 The selling life-cycle paradigm.

Sales Pipeline

Today   Tomorrow   Next Year   Next Decade

FIGURE 4-2 Rejection as part of the sales process.

A "no!"   repositions your   future
today   prospect in your   date.
             sales pipeline to a

The Selling Life-Cycle Paradigm also teaches us that there is little, if anything, you can do to force a prospect to buy. Therefore, you can maximize your return on investment by rapidly finding those prospects who are ready, willing, and able to buy now, while repositioning those who are not to an appropriate place in your sales pipeline.

In fact, this is one of the most asked questions in my prospecting seminar, "Red-Hot Cold Call Selling™, the Seminar." I am always asked how salespeople can speed up the sales cycle.

The honest answer is that you cannot speed up the sale. You can work efficiently, and I suppose this will speed up the sales cycle, but, assuming that you are working as efficiently as possible, you really cannot do any better than that. I suppose you could speed up the sales cycle by lowering your price, but any quality salesperson views this as an option of last resort.

Keep the Sales Pipeline Full

Given that you are working efficiently and given that you are not a price seller, the best strategy here is to have a full sales pipeline. In fact, whenever I get asked the question "How can I speed up the sales cycle?" I immediately ask to see the person's or company's sales pipeline. Prior to seeing the pipeline, I am willing to wager that the pipeline is insufficient to cover sales goals.

In case you are wondering what a sufficient pipeline should be, I would recommend sales goal coverage of 3X or more. What this means is that if your sales goal is $500,000 per quarter, you should have a "real" sales pipeline of $1.5 million if you hope to reach your sales goals on a consistent basis. This is not to say that if your pipeline is less than 3X, you will not achieve your goal. It's possible, but the odds are against you.

Since the magnitude of your pipeline is largely a function of your effort in the prospecting area, the magnitude of your pipeline is largely within your control. If you implement the ideas presented in this book, you will have, on average, a robust pipeline. If you do not implement the ideas in this book, you will run a significant risk that your pipeline, on average, may be insufficient to reach your sales goals.

Note that you need to have a *real* pipeline of 3X. What do I mean by *real*?

In measuring the magnitude of your sales pipeline, you must be honest with yourself and your company, and you must be realistic in your assessment of the opportunities in your sales pipeline. I see, all too often, salespeople carrying opportunities over from one quarter to the next. Did you know that new opportunities entered into your sales pipeline this quarter are three times more likely to close than opportunities carried over from quarter to quarter?

Prospecting, or attainment of your sales goals, is not an area about which to be fooling yourself or your company in order to defer the pressure of meeting your sales goals until after the close of the quarter. Prospecting is simply a function of desire and hard work, and you have the capacity for both. Why not maximize your value as a sales professional by simply doing the best you can? It is far better than consistently going through the month-end or quarter-end dance with your manager about whether or not you will achieve your sales goals.

In the next chapter, entitled "Smart Prospecting," we are going to discuss how to properly define your target market. You will learn that once prospects are in your target market, they will never leave your pipeline because your target market will be defined based on objective, quantitative criteria, not emotion. Therefore, a "no" today leaves you with no alternative but to reposition the prospect to an appropriate, new place in your sales pipeline. As long as your prospects meet the criteria that define your target market, they must remain in the sales pipeline, irrespective of the outcome of your last call to them. The emotion of rejection has been replaced with an objective, quantifiable criterion.

Remember: It's About Educating Your Prospect

I'd like to illustrate this point with an example. Not too long ago, one of our salespeople came to me looking a little disturbed and wondering what to do. He had just received a letter from Jan, one of his prospects in his target market, and wanted to discuss it with me. The letter said that we should stop calling the account, stop sending letters to the account, and remove the company from our mailing list. In fact, Jan wrote that we would never do business with the prospect account as long as she was the decision maker. The salesperson wanted to know what to do.

As I ripped up the letter, I referred the salesperson to the Selling Life-Cycle Paradigm: sales is a process, not an event. In fact, sales is an education process, and my interpretation of this event was that we simply had not done a good enough job in educating this prospect on the benefits of working with our organization.

The salesperson wanted to know why I was ripping up the letter. I replied, "When you call the prospect the next time, you will not remember how rude she had been to you." We simply removed the rejection element from the equation, focused on the facts (that is, that the prospect was still in our target market on the basis of our established criteria), and continued the sales process.

Over time, Jan left her company, and we wound up doing business with the prospect. Over the years, I have learned that if you give up, the outcome of the sales process is certain. You will never get the business. If you keep trying through the prospecting process that we are discussing in this chapter, at least you have a chance. You never know; you may actually win the business.

The name of the game in sales is to focus on what you can control (such as the effort you place into the sales process) and not to spend an inordinate amount of time on what you cannot control (such as the timing of the customer purchase decision). If you focus on your sales pipeline and the effort you place into the prospecting process, you will have a large pipeline, and you will find that you always will have opportunities maturing at the right time. If you focus on your sales pipeline, you will find that you no longer have the time to focus on rejection. You will be too busy trying to manage your success.

Becoming rejection-proof is one area that will allow you to get that competitive edge we were talking about in Chapter 1. The point to understand is that if you improve your probability of success on the margin over a large number of accounts, by believing in the Selling Life-Cycle Paradigm, you will have a tremendous impact on your success as a salesperson. Remember, the difference between Jack Nicklaus and Bob Charles was less than half a stroke per round.

Persistence Pays Off

I'm sure you have heard over and over again that most sales are made after the fifth sales call, yet most salespeople quit after the first call. In my opinion, the reason we quit can be traced back to our fear of rejection. Persistence, or not quitting after the first rejection, is one of the qualities that define not only successful salespeople but successful people in general. We are going to discuss the virtue of persistence in depth when we learn about the "10 Commandments of Prospecting" (see Chapter 6), but it may pay at this point to reflect upon some of the great examples of persistence that permeate our history books.

Many of us have heard how Abraham Lincoln lost every election but one prior to his being elected president of the United States. Where would he (and the United States) have wound up if it were not for his persistence?

Many of us have also read how Thomas Edison failed more than 10,000 times prior to inventing the incandescent light. However, Edison's view of failure can shed interesting light on the word *persistence*. Rather than defining what had happened as failure, he believed that he had succeeded in finding 10,000 ways not to invent the incandescent light. In other words, the process of elimination is a vital part of the invention process. Edison went on to say that he knew he would soon succeed because he had run out of ways that didn't work. Where would we be today if it were not for Edison's great persistence?

More recent history also points to great examples of persistence. Colonel Sanders was rejected more than a thousand times before his first successful sale of the Kentucky Fried Chicken formula. Lee Iacocca was fired from the presidency of Ford Motor Company, but his persistence led him on to even greater heights as the chairman of Chrysler Corporation.

Thomas Watson, the founder of IBM, when asked how others could emulate his great success formula, replied simply that they should increase their rate of failure. In other words, trying and failing is a risk one must bear in order to be able to try and succeed. Why? Because failure and rejection are necessary precursors to success. Watson's formula works only when combined with one additional special ingredient—persistence.

You cannot lose the game if you control when it ends. Viewing selling as a process and not an event allows you to control the end of the game. Make sure it ends only after you convert the prospect to a satisfied client.

I've often said, "It's only a matter of time before everyone in the world will do business with me." While I might sound a little overconfident, I'm simply reinforcing the Selling Life-Cycle Paradigm. I control when the game ends, I persist, I continue to educate my prospects, and ultimately they will understand the superior value my product or service brings to their organization.

Overcoming the Fear of Rejection Through Diversification

In Chapter 2, we discussed the Law of Sowing and Reaping. This law suggests that whatever we soweth, so shall we reapeth. When we expanded this definition to cover prospecting, we learned that our cold calls are the seeds that we plant at the beginning of the sales cycle. Plant only one seed, and your whole harvest depends on the outcome of that one seed. Make only one cold call, and your whole selling career depends on the outcome of that one cold call. If your whole selling career depends on the outcome of only one call, it becomes quite clear why prospecting can be a great source of anxiety for the salesperson. Hence, the fear of rejection.

The key to removing this anxiety or fear lies in the fact that you must make enough prospecting calls so that the outcome of one call is not and cannot be significant to your overall selling results. This strategy is not new in business, but it may not have received its due in selling. The strategy is called *diversification*.

In the financial community, mutual funds were created to achieve diversification. Invest in one stock, and your financial well-being rests with the fortunes of just one company as the stock price goes either up or down. A mutual fund, in contrast, is a collection of stocks. In fact, it's typically a large collection of stocks. The theory behind mutual fund investing is that the movement in any one stock has very little impact on the overall results of the fund. In other words, you have diversified away your risk. If you feel that investing in one mutual fund is still too risky, you could diversify even more by investing in several mutual funds, further reducing the effect any one stock could have on your investments' overall financial performance.

Prospecting can work in exactly the same manner. As you increase the number of cold calls you make, the outcome of any one call has less and less significance. Couple this strategy with the Selling Life-Cycle Paradigm, which suggests that it's only a matter of time before every prospect will do business with you, and you should be able to remove prospecting anxiety and the fear of rejection completely from your vocabulary.

Applying the theory of diversification to your day-to-day selling activities can be very revealing. In Chapter 2, we defined a relationship between dials of the telephone and sales volume. I told you that this relationship was as predictable as the sun rising in the East and setting in the West. The reason I can be so sure of this relationship is that it is based on the Law of Large Numbers. In fact, the entire insurance industry, and the entire selling profession, is based on this same law. Actuaries can tell you how many males in the state of New York between the ages of 25 and 35 will have car accidents this year. The thing they cannot tell you is which ones. Prospecting works in exactly the same manner. Using myself as an example, I know that I will get one appointment, on average, every 10 times I dial the phone. Remember, a dial is defined as simply pressing the requisite phone number and letting the phone ring. What I can't tell you is who the appointments will be with.

Please keep in mind that this does not mean I get one appointment each and every time I make 10 dials. Sometimes I get more, and sometimes I get none. On average, though, I do get one in 10, and I can bank on it. Because I understand that over the long run I will achieve the results that I am looking for, one rejection, or many rejections, has no impact whatsoever on my mental attitude.

You, too, have your own ratio that you can bank on. This is the most compelling reason to keep track of your prospecting activities. So, if you ever fear rejection, if you ever have anxiety surrounding the cold-calling process, understand that the source of your anxiety stems from the simple fact that you are not making enough calls. You are violating the Law of Sowing and Reaping and the Law of Large Numbers. The good news is that now you have a cure for your anxiety: Make more calls!

Believe in Your Product; Believe in Yourself

Before we close this chapter, I have two final thoughts on rejection-proof prospecting. First, I have taught professional selling to thousands of students over the years. While the names, faces, companies, and products change, there is always one constant. Virtually all my students firmly believe that they are benefiting their customer or prospect by selling them their product or service. In other words, they believe in their product or service. If they didn't believe in their product or service, they would have great difficulty being successful and would have likely moved on to another sales position.

If you believe in your product or service, each time you make a sale you are making your customer better off. If you believe that your customers are better off for having done business with you, doesn't it make sense that your prospects will also be better off? Of course it does! Keep this in mind during the prospecting process. Most salespeople believe they are being a bother to prospects by repeatedly calling to arrange for an appointment. If you believe in your product or service, your perspective should be just the opposite. You should feel as though you have an obligation to call your prospects. Remember, you are selling a good and improving the prospect's position by making a purchase with you. Knowing that you are providing a much-needed product or service to the marketplace should enhance your confidence and move you closer to your goal of becoming rejection-proof.

Finally, remember that you cannot lose what you never had, so let's not lament the seeds that do not grow. Rather, let's move on to the next chapter, "Smart Prospecting," which will add to our rejection-proof strategies, as well as teach us how to work smarter, not harder.

CHAPTER 5

Smart Prospecting

We have talked quite a bit about maximizing your return on investment as a sales professional. In order to do this, we must understand that all salespeople are created equal. In other words, we are all given the same commodity to invest each and every day: time. Not only are we given the same commodity with which to trade, but we are all given equal amounts: 24 hours in a day. It stands to reason that a salesperson who invests his time most wisely will receive the highest return on his investment. In fact, the name of the game in selling, and in business, is to maximize your return on investment. For a salesperson, return on investment is calculated as:

$$\text{Return on investment} = \frac{\text{Sale}}{\text{Time invested in the sale}}$$

Fishing for Whales

In Chapter 1, we reviewed a sample sales cycle. The sales cycle included planning, prospecting, meeting, recommending, closing, and servicing. When we reviewed the sales cycle, we noted that you could start the sales cycle at step 2, the prospecting step, without considering step 1, the planning step. While this is true, I believe that planning should be a necessary precursor to prospecting. The equation tells us that a salesperson's return on investment is calculated by taking the value of a sale and dividing it by the time invested in the sale. The time invested in a sale is does not vary significantly with the size of the sale. In other words, as the magnitude of the sale increases, the time one needs to close the sales does not increase in proportion to the sale size.

Therefore, in order to maximize your return on investment, you will have to maximize the magnitude of your sale. In order to maximize your return on investment as a salesperson, you must find those buyers of your products and services that are most likely to make major purchases. And this requires planning.

To illustrate my point, let's consider two car buyers: one a wealthy buyer looking to purchase a very expensive car, and the other a middle-class buyer looking to borrow money to purchase a moderate car that will be paid off over a three-year period.

The wealthy buyer will likely purchase the car without too much investigation. Why? First, the purchase is not that significant to the wealthy buyer. Second, a very expensive car probably has an assumed level of quality.

On the other hand, the middle-class buyer will probably invest many hours understanding her purchase decision. Why? The purchase is very significant to the middle-class buyer. It is one she will have to live with for three years. Second, given her limited resources, the middle-class buyer will likely investigate the purchase in greater detail to make certain she is maximizing her return on investment.

This example would argue that smaller purchasers invest more time in a purchase decision than do large buyers. This is probably true for individual purchasers. But what about corporate purchasers? Would they follow the same rule of thumb?

Corporations are in business to make money, or, to continue with the return-on-investment analogy, to maximize their return on investment. Given this fact, I suggest that corporate purchasers, with a mandate to maximize their return on investment, will invest a similar amount of time in a purchase decision, irrespective of the size of the purchase. After all, have you ever worked with someone who said,

"Don't be concerned with doing a good job for us since we are only a small purchaser of your product or service"? Of course you haven't.

The key point to understanding our return-on-investment equation is this: If the time you must invest in a sale is not going to vary significantly irrespective of the size of the sale, you must maximize the size of the sale in order to maximize your return on investment. This brings us to the first rule in smart prospecting: Fish for whales and not for minnows!

After presenting this unique way of viewing the purchase decision in many seminars, I often hear an objection from seminar participants who say fishing for whales is akin to "putting all of your eggs in one basket." That is, if you only have a few large accounts and you lose one, you will lose a significant portion of your income.

Just remember that you can always mitigate your risk by having more than a few large accounts. This is the benefit of account diversity and the Law of Sowing and Reaping, discussed in Chapter 2.

Enterprise Versus Territory Account Management

When you look at account executives in the context of territory management, you will see that there are two types of account executives: enterprise account managers and territory account managers.

An enterprise account manager is an account manager dedicated to cultivating the largest accounts in the market for a particular company. Here, you might find that the account manager has only a few, or even one account on his account list. A good example of an enterprise account would be General Electric, ABN AMRO Bank in Europe (The Netherlands), or Samsung in Asia (Korea). Enterprise accounts are the crème de la crème of corporations in your geography. The reason that you have only one or a few accounts on your account list is that these accounts are so large; you would not have the time to properly service an enterprise account and service or prospect to the many other accounts on your account list. Working with General Electric, ABN AMRO, or Samsung is a full-time job. If these accounts are on your list, you probably do not have time to do much else but properly service or cultivate these accounts.

If you are in this situation, where you only have one or two extremely large accounts on your account list, you might be wondering how the benefits of account diversity and the Law of Sowing and Reaping apply to you.

Believe it or not, enterprise account managers and territory managers have very similar roles in terms of covering their enterprise accounts or territories. Let's see why.

A territory account manager is one who manages all of the smaller accounts in a geographic region. For example, if you were an account executive in New York City, you might have as your territory all of the smaller accounts in the Wall Street district. Or you might have all of the smaller accounts in midtown Manhattan. Midtown Manhattan could even be subdivided into the East Side and the West Side, since there are so many companies in Manhattan to cover.

The key point here is that the enterprise accounts are the largest accounts in the market. These are specifically assigned to the enterprise account managers. Once the enterprise accounts are assigned, this leaves the relatively smaller accounts in the market or in the territory.

The reason that the smaller accounts are typically divided by geographic territory is time management. You will be more time efficient if you work in a smaller geographic region.

A third way to divide accounts is by industry. Dividing accounts by industry is also a smart thing to consider because of the specialized knowledge required to work within a particular industry, such as insurance. Once an account executive takes the time to learn a particular industry, it is also not time efficient to have a second account manager repeat the learning process unless there are enough accounts within both the industry and the territory to support two account managers. It is much more time efficient to leverage someone's expertise in a particular industry than to require that all account managers acquire the same level of expertise.

Please note that within a particular industry segment you can still have enterprise accounts and territory accounts. Please also note that from a management perspective, it would not be a good idea to vest *all* of your industry knowledge in one individual because this would be very risky from a business perspective. From a risk management point of view, it would be better to have a primary industry expert and a secondary industry expert. What you would not want to do is have everyone in the sales organization duplicate this specialized level of expertise.

So, let's get back to our discussion about territory and enterprise account managers. I noted that their roles, from a new business development perspective, are similar. A territory account manager manages the smaller accounts within a specific geographic region. An enterprise account manager manages one to maybe five of the larger accounts in the region. So, where are the similarities? A territory account executive has many accounts and an enterprise account manager has only one or a few accounts.

Actually, an enterprise account is really more than one account. Let's take a look at GE, for example.

When I last analyzed GE from a new business development or prospecting perspective, I found that GE was not one account at all. In fact, I found that GE was divided into six major business segments: Commercial Finance, Consumer Finance, Healthcare, Industrial, Infrastructure, and NBC Universal.

Within each business segment, there were a number of what would otherwise be called companies, if these GE businesses were not part of the GE family. If you took a look at the Commercial Finance, for example, you would find five different companies, including Corporate Financial Services and Healthcare Financial Services. When I did the work on GE, what I found was that GE was made up of 32 distinct businesses (e.g., Corporate Financial Services and Healthcare Financial Services) across the six different business segments.

If you were the account executive for GE, prior to reading this chapter, you might think that you had one account on your account list. What I have just shown you is that you really have 32 accounts on your account list. These 32 accounts are the 32 distinct businesses across the six business segments just discussed.

If you were to then look into Corporate Financial Services, for example, in more depth, you would find that Corporate Financial Services has six businesses. Among these six businesses are Corporate Lending and Bank Loan Group. Using Corporate Financial Services as an example and as an average, you could argue that each of the 32 major GE businesses has (on average) six subbusinesses (as does Corporate Financial Services). Clearly, some businesses will have more subbusinesses and some will have fewer. Even my assumption of six subbusinesses, on average, may be wrong. But the point I am trying to make is just as significant whether the average number of subbusinesses for each GE businesses is three, four, five, or six. Again, using six as an average, you can easily see that GE has now grown from 32 accounts for new business development purposes to 192 accounts (32 x 6) for new business development purposes.

And, I hope you are sitting down because your work does not end here!

Now that you have 192 accounts in your list, you must consider geographies, regions, countries, locations, and so on. What I am trying to point out here is that the decision making in Asia might not be the same decision making in North America. So, accounting for the three geographies in the world—the Americas (Canada through South America), EMEA (Europe, the Middle East, and Africa), and Asia—you have just increased your account list to 576 (192 x 3 geographies) potential accounts.

And, before you put down my book in utter surprise, I am going to take you one level deeper into the account analysis. The final level that we need to consider is actual contacts or people to call. You should have at least several contacts per account; the true decision makers, end users, technical decision makers, purchasing contacts, line of business executives, and others. So assuming five contacts per account, you now have a contact list of 2,880 contacts.

While this may surprise you, it should not. This is what you need to do to cover an account like GE. In my personal domain, IBM is my largest personal account. At IBM, I have well over 400 contacts, and I have been working with IBM for about five years. While one could say I am doing a good job, I look at it from another perspective.

If there are 1,000 people I need to know at IBM, and I know only 400 of them, there is still a lot of work to do (and there is still a lot of potential!) at IBM.

So, you should be able to see at this point that irrespective of whether you are an enterprise account manager or a territory account manager, there is a lot of business development work that needs to be done. Account diversity and the Law of Sowing and Reaping are equally applicable to enterprise account managers and territory account managers.

Sources for Account Research and Planning

When conducting research, I use two resources to obtain information. One is the company's Web site, and the second is OneSource (www .onesource.com).

In general, a company's Web site will provide you with lots of useful information about the company from a new business development perspective. So will OneSource. I prefer OneSource because it is more time efficient and more in depth, but the corporate Web site is also a good resource.

OneSource aggregates information from a number of other information portals and provides you with the information in one location (hence the name OneSource). Perhaps the most useful feature in OneSource is that it provides you with the "corporate family."

OneSource happens to be a U.S. resource, though it is global in scope. As you might expect, the quality of the information provided diminishes as you move farther and farther from the United States. If the OneSource information is not adequate for my purposes, then I resort to the corporate Web site. It is more time consuming than OneSource, but gathering of this information is not really optional from a sales and prospecting perspective.

I use Factiva (www.factiva.com), another research resource, to alert me to major changes at the account.

Factiva scans more than 8,000 media resources each day. These resources range from global resources such as the *Wall Street Journal*,

CNN, and the BBC to local resources such as the local news paper in Sao Paulo, Brazil. Factiva probably includes your local news sources and also includes industrial journals such as Chemical Week.

To use Factiva, you establish a "Factiva Track," with the company names of the companies you wish to cover. When your account shows up in a media journal, Factiva notifies you via e-mail. So, if GE reorganized its corporate structure and this information was reported in a media source, Factiva would make me aware of the change within one day (not one business day, as Factiva works on the weekend as well).

Factiva is also useful for new contact information. If, for example, a new Chief Information Officer or Vice President of Sales were appointed at one of your accounts, Factiva would make you aware of this in a timely manner (one day as well). This is obviously very useful information for prospecting purposes.

As long as we are on the topic of market intelligence or research resources, I have already introduced you to three key resources: the company Web site, OneSource, and Factiva. I want to complete the topic and introduce you to a few more.

The first resource I want to introduce you to is Hoovers (www .hoovers.com). I use Hoovers for two reasons. The first reason is to get summary financial data. Hoovers is excellent for this. It provides you with two-year trends for sales growth, net income growth, and employee growth. You can easily use this information to enhance your prospecting efforts.

We are going to talk about scripting in Chapter 7, but developing a good prospecting script is crucial to your success. If, for example, you notice that a company's sales are decreasing and your solution could have a positive impact on this problem, you could call the appropriate person in the target account and say, "The reason I am calling is that I was reviewing your corporate financial statements on Hoovers and noticed that your sales decreased by 10 percent year over year. I'm sure this is of concern to you, and our solution can have a major positive impact on your sales results."

While developing a good prospecting script is a bit more complicated than this, you should be able to see that at least you have a great reason to make a call. I'm sure you are aware that if you do not believe that you have a valid reason for the call, you will be far less likely to call.

A second, additional resource that I want to point you to is Google (www.google.com). Many of the resources I am discussing are American-centric. They work best in the United States. These resources should also work fairly well in Canada and Western Europe. However, as you get farther and farther away from the United States, the effectiveness of these resources may diminish.I am not going to say that these resources will not work in South America, Eastern Europe, or Asia. What I am going to say is that the resources *may not* work.

Google, as you probably know, is one of the world's most popular search engines. If I were in Korea, for example, and I needed information about one particular company, I would use the corporate Web site. If I were in Korea and I needed information about the top companies in Korea for territory planning purposes, I would use Google.

Go to Google and type in "Companies in Korea." What Google will return to you is a list of the Korean (i.e., local) business resources and lists that you can use or purchase (in some cases) to get a firm understanding of the sales landscape in Korea.

There are three other resource points that I want to make before we move on.

The first point is that there are often specialized industry resources that may also be useful to your sales and prospecting efforts. Our company does a lot of work in the technology sector with companies like IBM, Applied Materials, Sybase, and Parametric Technology Corporation.

One technology resource that a technology salesperson can use is called Harte-Hanks (www.harte-hanks.com). Harte-Hanks provides you with the technology landscape of a particular corporation. By using Harte-Hanks, you can find out what hardware is installed at an account, what software is installed at an account, and what outsourced technology business services are used at an account, and, often, you can learn about a company's technology strategy and direction. This should be useful information for any technology sales or business development professional.

While I cannot claim to have worked in every industry in the world, my judgment leads me to believe that similar resources exist for many major industries.

The next point that I want to make is this: "Don't forget to look right under your nose." Your own company should have an internal database that can provide you with useful market intelligence resources. Also, don't forget others in the company, even if they work in different product silos. Business partners and vendors can also be a useful source of market intelligence information.

Finally, much of the research we have discussed relates to markets or companies. As a business developer, you need to call people. Hoovers, OneSource, Factiva, the corporate Web site, and industry resources such as Harte-Hanks can all be used to provide contacts for you to call at a particular account.

You should be able to see, at this point, that your research opportunities are vast. Research is part of the job of any great sales professional. There is always a significant, upfront investment in research. It is important that you understand that this is a one-time investment used to "get you into the sales game." After that, much smaller amounts of research can be done to supplement and enhance the results of your original research investment.

Accuracy of Information

There is no perfect information source. However, the lack of a perfect research source does not invalidate the need to perform research. What do you think will yield a better result—no research at all or research resources that are (only) 70, 80, or 90 percent perfect? Since I usually ask rhetorical questions in my books, I will not answer this question for you either.

Frequency of Research

When I consider research, I consider it an upfront investment that is required to enter the sales business. If you were to start almost any business, you would likely need to make an investment. Research is the investment that you need to make to enter the sales business. The majority of the investment is made at the beginning of your career and needs to be repeated en masse only if your territory, account list, or company of employment changes. So, all of the analysis that that was performed for General Electric should last for quite some time. I do not need to repeat this analysis on a monthly, quarterly, or even annual basis. Rather, I do the analysis once and then continue to add to it over time.

I have used all of the resources discussed in this chapter all over the world. We have a global client base in our business, and, where appropriate, I will make comments about what changes as you leave the United States and go to other countries.

The Sales Portfolio

In the field of investing, a portfolio is the collection of all of your stocks. In the field of professional selling, a portfolio is the collection of all of your customers or accounts. When you make investments, you get to set the level of risk you wish to bear. If you wish to bear more risk, you invest in fewer stocks. If you wish to bear less risk, you invest in more stocks, thus diversifying away some of your risk.

The same can be said of your sales portfolio. You get to set your level of risk! If you wish to have a high-risk portfolio, you make investments in fewer accounts. If you wish to have a lower-risk portfolio, you can also diversify away a portion of your risk by investing in more accounts.

I want to stop for a moment at this point and remind you that, for most businesses, you can have as many accounts as you wish. Clearly, if you are a territory account manager with a number of accounts in your territory, this is true.

Also, if you are an enterprise account manager, with an account like GE, and your product or service can be used by the many different segments of GE, as outlined earlier, this is also true. Remember, at GE, we suggested that you might have more than 200 accounts and more than 1,000 contacts if you fully covered the GE account. So, you could elect to place yourself in a risky position and work only with GE

Corporate Headquarters, or, as I would recommend, you may want to diversify away the risk of working only with the corporate headquarters location and start to branch out into the different businesses as I outlined earlier.

There are a few industries, such as the semiconductor equipment manufacturing industry, with companies like Applied Materials and Lam Research, to which my diversification theory does not apply. Companies like Applied Materials and Lam Research sell equipment that makes chips to companies like Intel and AMD, large global chip manufacturers.

The equipment sold by companies like Applied Materials is typically very large and very expensive, and there are only a few companies in the world (like Intel and AMD) that buy this type of equipment.

The last time I looked, there were only 200 or 300 companies in the world that would buy a specific type of equipment sold by either Applied or Lam. Yes, it is true that Intel may have a number of chip manufacturing locations, and there might be multiple purchase or sales opportunities at Intel, but even considering this, it would be very hard to diversify away the risk inherent in having a small sales portfolio. There is simply not much that a seller can do in this industry from a prospecting perspective. On the other hand, a seller in this industry is not likely to be reading this book because her need to hone her prospecting skills is simply not that significant. A skill such as value selling is much more important to a company like Applied.

In general, you can assume that it is possible to diversify away that risk of having only a few accounts in your sales portfolio. In fact, I suggest (again) that this is your number one sales strategy. I have said this before in this book, and I will say it again. The number one sales strategy in the world, bar none, is to have a full sales pipeline. One way to achieve that is through prospecting. Through prospecting, you should be able to make the outcome of any one sales transaction or any customer, for that matter, insignificant to your overall sales results and sales career. Wouldn't it be great not to have to lower your price to close a deal? Or wouldn't it be great not to be able to select from among three or more customers on the basis of which one will offer you the best business terms? I know that these may seem like farfetched dreams, but they are not. This is why you are reading this book!

So, there is no reason to believe that you can manage only a few (large) accounts. You can manage as many as you wish, thus setting the level of risk you wish to bear. How do you find these large accounts? Well, that's exactly what we are going to discuss next!

Defining Your Target Market

What I am about to show you may be the best thing you will ever learn in your sales career. It certainly has been for me and for the many clients that have implemented it.

When I started my first company, in 1983, we were able to grow the company from zero in sales and no customers in the beginning to a company with approximately $100 million in sales over a 12-year career. Most people who read this story would say that this is a good accomplishment. I suppose that I would, too; however, the results would have been far more dramatic if I had only known about "Smart Prospecting."

The first step in Smart Prospecting involves defining your target market.

Most salespeople might define their target market as "all companies that purchase our product or service." Or, if you work within a region, you might refine your definition to focus on your region only.

The concern with the previous definition is the word *all*. The word *all* implies a lack of focus. Remember, our goal as salespeople is to maximize our return on investment, and we can accomplish this goal only by finding those buyers of our product or service who are most likely to make major purchases. Although it might seem as though you are limiting your opportunities by excluding some buyers from your target market, you are not. What you are doing is setting your priorities so that you work with the largest and most likely buyers in your market first. You can always expand your target market definition at a later time to include additional buyers. However, you would want to expand only after you had first worked with all potential buyers in your initial target market definition.

My experience has been that if you properly define your target market, there will be sufficient opportunity within it so that it will not be worth your while to look outside your target market. The opportunities outside your target market will simply be too small. More important, you will have maximized the return you receive on the time you invest in the sales process.

Instead of defining your target market with the word *all*, you might consider defining your target market on the basis of a demographic factor. The demographic factor you select should be the one that best describes the buying potential of your target market. Examples might be gross sales of the target prospect, number of locations, number of employees, and net worth for individuals.

For example, by selecting all companies with more than 100 employees or all individuals with a net worth in excess of $100,000, you will have separated the large buyers of your product or service from the smaller buyers. In selecting your demographic factor, you should consider one that is easily obtained. After all, you do not want to spend all of your time doing research and none of your time selling.

You might be wondering where one obtains the necessary demographics to perform the exercise of Smart Prospecting. You should know that we have already answered this question. Since this is such a crucial step for you, let me outline the steps one by one:

1. Go to Hoovers to determine your target market. Hoovers allows you to search companies on several criteria, including gross sales, employee count, industry, and geographic region. Start with your region, and then select your companies either by gross sales or employee count (cross industry focus) or by industry (industry focus). You will have to decide if a cross-industry or industry focus is best for you.

2. Whether you select an industry or cross-industry focus, you will next need to review the data to determine if you can work with all of the companies you have selected or a particular subset. You usually want to work with a subset if your resources are limited (i.e., there are too many accounts in the

target market to handle), or if your solutions are targeted to a specific market segment, such as the small and medium business market. At the end of step two, you will have a specific, manageable set of accounts that you can focus on.

3. While you are in Hoovers, make sure to gather the contact information, the line-of-business information, and the summary financial information that Hoovers provides.

4. If you are in a region of the world where Hoovers does not provide sufficiently good data, remember to use Google to find a business resource in your region that does.

5. Now that you are done with Hoovers and have a defined target market, you will want to use OneSource to understand the lines of business at your accounts. This is particularly useful if the companies that you are working are in the moderate to enterprise market segment. Moderately large and large companies will almost always have different lines of business that you need to consider.

6. If you work with smaller companies, OneSource may be too much of a resource for you. In this case, use the companies' Web sites, which you can access free of charge.

7. While you are using OneSource, please also make use of the contact information there. OneSource will provide you with multiple line-of-business contacts at each of the different business segments within your accounts.

8. After you are done with OneSource, move over to Factiva and set up a Factiva track for the accounts in your target market. Again, this will cost you a bit of money, but I think it is well worth the money spent. If you simply cannot afford the financial investment, you can always do this manually by using either Yahoo! or Google.

9. The next step in the process is to use an industry-specific resource such as Harte-Hanks for the technology industry to look at your accounts from a technical perspective. Think of a

resource such as Harte-Hanks as the alter ego of a resource such as Hoovers. Hoovers focuses on the financial and business side of the equation, and Harte-Hanks focuses on the technical side of the equation, providing you with technical contacts, technical strategy, and technical usage.

10. The last step in the process is to review your internal corporate resources, including other sellers and people within your company. Do not overlook the information that is provided for you within your own company.

As you can see, whenever you are searching for information, you can always find it from one of two sources: purchased sources and free sources. Great examples of purchased information are the ones that we have already discussed in depth: Hoovers, Harte-Hanks, One-Source, and Factiva. The big benefit of purchased information is that someone else has taken the time to cull through countless mounds of data and refined the data into an immediately useful format for the salesperson. The big detriment to purchased information is it requires financial resources that might not be available to the salesperson.

There are also a number of sources of free information, including corporate Web sites, Google, Yahoo!, and other Internet sites. You can also go to the local Chamber of Commerce, the public library, and your city's trade or business publication. The major benefit of free information is that it does not require a financial investment in order to be of use. The major detriment is that it does require a significant investment in time to raise the quality of the free information to the level of purchased information.

The question one is faced with is, once again, where one can obtain the greatest return on investment. Where the financial resources exist, my personal bias would be for purchased information. I believe that purchasing good information and focusing your efforts on selling will usually lead to a higher return on investment. Where the purchased information is not a likely alternative, using free information and sifting through it using your human capital will serve as a nice surrogate.

Continuing with our example and assuming that the number of employees is the demographic factor that best describes your target market, you could fine-tune the definition of your target market from "all companies that could use our product or service" to "all companies with more than 100 employees that could use our product or service." In my business, we have made the decision that 100 employees separates the large purchasers from the smaller purchasers, since our demographic factor is designed to quantify the buying potential of prospects within our target market.

A number of our clients that have implemented this approach have dubbed it the "Large Account Strategy." In the example, we are going to call on the companies with more than 100 employees, that is, the large accounts. Hence, the name "Large Account Strategy."

While this is a good name and a great strategy, I do not want to imply that this strategy does not work for companies that focus on the small and medium business market. It most certainly does.

Let's say that you are working in the small and medium business space and are calling on companies with one to 100 employees, not companies with more than 100 employees. If this is the case, the Large Account Strategy still applies.

First, it will still pay for you to complete most, if not all, of the 10 steps just outlined. This will give you a great understanding of your market, which is one of my foremost objectives here.

Second, within your small and medium business market, there are still larger accounts and smaller accounts. This is true whether you are focusing on an account with less than 100 employees or accounts with more than 100 employees. In any market, there are larger and smaller accounts. It not only pays to know who are the larger and smaller accounts in your target market, it also pays to have a comprehensive list of all (or as close to all as possible) of the accounts in your target market.

All too often, I see great accounts that are not on an account list and should be. I have worked with companies where the largest account in the market somehow is not on their account list. I have also worked with companies where many of the top 10 accounts in the market are not on their account list.

If an account is not on your list, how do you expect to win a sale at the account? You can't! If you are not working the account, your likelihood of winning a sale at the company drops pretty close to zero. I always say that part of the prospecting process is "just getting invited to the party." If you are outside the United States and don't understand what I mean by getting invited to the party, it simply means that you cannot win a sale if you are not part of the proposal process.

So, Smart Prospecting or the Large Account Strategy applies irrespective of your target market. An additional benefit of the Large Account Strategy is that residence in your target market is now determined by an objective criterion, not your feelings toward the prospect. In other words, as long as the prospect has 100 or more employees (going back to our main example), it remains in your target market, and you must continue to cultivate the relationship.

Alternatively, if you have a poorly defined target market, rejection often will serve as a surrogate for your demographic factor, which means that your feelings toward the prospect, not buying potential, will determine how you set your priorities. I suggest that buying potential (the objective criterion), not feelings toward the prospect derived from numerous rejections (the subjective criterion) be the determining factor in how you set priorities within your target market. This will serve to make you rejection-proof, since your emotions will now be removed from the equation, and will maximize your return on investment, since you will be basing your decisions on buying potential.

If you reflect back to the Selling Life-Cycle Paradigm, you will now better understand why "it's just a matter of time before everyone in the world will do business with you!" By defining your target market as any company with 100 or more employees, you, as the salesperson, cannot decide whether or not a company qualifies for your target market. An objective demographic factor is the controlling variable. Therefore, a company or individual cannot reject itself out of your target market. Only a change in the demographic factor can. Combine the Selling Life-Cycle Paradigm with a healthy dose of persistence, and you'll be on your way to prospecting success.

Another benefit of defining your target market in a quantitative fashion is the benefit of focus. Les Brown, the famous motivational speaker, says that you are either moving toward your goals or away from them. There is no in-between, because even if you are standing still, the rest of the world is moving forward. Hence, you are being left behind. By defining your target market in a quantitative manner, there is no doubt whether a prospect is in or out. This allows you to focus only on those accounts that are in your target market. In other words, you're always moving toward your goal of maximizing your return on investment because you are working only with the largest buyers of your product or service in the marketplace.

Our analysis, thus far, is strictly quantitative, very black and white. However, there are two additional factors that you may want to consider when formulating your target market: geography and one additional demographic factor.

Geography is important in many industries. If this is true in your industry, the closer you are to a customer, the more likely you are to do business with him. This factor probably relates back to your ability to service the customer and the customer's desire to see with whom he is doing business. If your business is one in which proximity to the customer plays a role in the decision-making process, you may want to consider adding a geographic dimension to your definition of a target market.

Continuing with our example, the definition of your target market could then be modified to be "all companies within 100 miles of our office and with more than 100 employees that could use our product or service."

I also said that you may want to add one additional demographic factor, such as the region's list of fastest-growing companies, to your definition of a target market to allow for some flexibility.

There are certain accounts in every market that are deemed to be "strategic," and you don't want to construct your definition so rigidly that you exclude those companies. Strategic accounts could be the region's list of fastest-growing companies or Fortune 2000 companies with locations in your geographic region, no matter what the size.

The reason the former might be considered strategic is that although these companies may not be in your target market today on the basis of your original target market definition, they may be the giants of tomorrow, so you may want to consider working with them now. The reason the latter might be considered strategic is your ability to leverage the relationship and use them as a reference at other accounts in your target market. Saying you do business with a high-profile company lends a great deal of credibility to a sales presentation.

The one concern with adding an additional element to your definition of a target market is that you must be careful not to dilute your focus. Otherwise, you'll wind up back to the *all* definition and lose your ability to set priorities.

Concluding our example, our final target market definition might be "all companies within 100 miles of our office and with more than 100 employees, or any company on our region's list of 50 fastest-growing companies, irrespective of how many employees they currently have, that could use our product or service."

In summary, notice that the definition of our target market includes the following elements:

❑ A quantitative element based on a known demographic factor

❑ A geographic element based on proximity to your office (if applicable)

❑ One additional quantitative element, used for strategic purposes, to provide for limited flexibility

Segmenting Your Target Market

Once you have defined your target market, the next step is to segment your market into three categories: high-priority accounts, moderate-priority accounts, and low-priority accounts. The goal here is to further refine your target market so that you place the greatest emphasis on those prospects that are most likely to buy the largest quantities of your product or service. This will, of course, result in maximizing your return on investment.

Your priorities should again be based on the demographic and geographic factors selected previously. For example, our target market could be stratified as follows:

❏ *High-Priority Accounts:* Any account with more than 250 employees within 50 miles of our office

❏ *Moderate-Priority Accounts:* Any account with 100 to 250 employees within 50 miles of our office or any account with more than 250 employees farther than 50 miles from our office

❏ *Low-Priority Accounts:* Any account with 100 to 250 employees farther than 50 miles from our office

The reason for stratifying your market is that you can now set call and visit goals for each account so as to place your greatest emphasis on those accounts that will maximize your return on investment. Again, referring to the Selling Life-Cycle Paradigm, the approach of stratifying your target market will ensure that you minimize the time between calls to your largest accounts. In turn, this will ensure that the largest potential accounts are consistently being placed into your sales pipeline.

Before discussing why and how to set call and visit goals, it is appropriate to discuss what happens to accounts outside your target market. For example, suppose a company with 50 employees calls up to place an order. Should you accept the order? The answer to this question is, of course, yes. However, the reason for the answer is that the company called you; you did not make the call. For accounts outside your target market, I suggest a less expensive strategy than face-to-face selling. These smaller accounts might be the target of a direct-mail campaign, for example. I would not recommend making them the focus of your telemarketing and face-to-face selling efforts, since they will not yield a return on investment sufficient to justify your efforts. A direct-mail program, with a lower investment per contact, may be sufficient to address this segment of the marketplace.

Goals for Your Target Market

I would now like to address how to set appropriate call and visit goals for each of your three target market segments.

In general, for goals to be effective as motivational devices, they must be achievable and within the control of the salesperson. The strength of call and visit goals are that call and visit goals are largely within the control of the salesperson. Each day, you can fully control the number of prospecting calls that you make. To a lesser extent, you can also control the number of client and prospect visits you make, largely by controlling your call activity.

An example of how one might set call and visit goals for each category of account in your target market follows:

- ❏ *High-Priority Accounts:* One call per month, one face-to-face visit per quarter
- ❏ *Moderate-Priority Accounts*: One call per quarter, one face-to-face visit per half-year
- ❏ *Low-Priority Accounts*: One call per half-year, one face-to-face visit per year

Winning with Smart Prospecting

The key point to understand is that your call and visit goals must reflect the priorities you established when you stratified your target market. The end result should be a prospecting plan that leaves no doubt what you, as a salesperson, must do in order to achieve market success. The final rule in Smart Prospecting is to make as many calls as possible.

This might sound like a contradiction, because quality calls should always be preferred to quantity calls. However, because you have taken the time to qualify and quantify your target market, each call you make is, by definition, a quality call. Therefore, the only remaining variable is quantity, or how much effort you want to put into your selling success.

At this point, you probably understand that Smart Prospecting is a significant element of your overall sales strategy. Smart Prospecting is designed to maximize your return on investment. In the next chapter, we are going to learn about the 10 Commandments of Prospecting, a series of additional prospecting strategies that will enhance your probability of success in the sales cycle.

CHAPTER 6

The 10 Commandments of Prospecting

Prospecting can be much like going to the health club. It's something that you know is good for you and will produce excellent and predictable results, yet it's something that most salespeople seem to avoid. When I reflect back on my first selling position, I was always busy but never seemed to prospect and hence, never seemed to sell. What we are going to propose in this chapter is a simple 10-step system that will help you in the prospecting process. While each step in the system may not seem to break new ground, it is the system itself that yields tremendous results.

A system is simply a proven methodology for accomplishing a goal. Years ago, I had a goal of losing some weight. I tried dieting on my own but was not successful. Then, I joined the Weight Watchers Weight Loss Program, followed its system, and was very successful. The difference in results came from the difference in the system. The interesting thing about the Weight Watchers system is that it worked with an amazing degree of accuracy and predictability. Those who followed the system lost weight; those who didn't had less success.

A further interesting observation is that only slight modifications to the system seemed to destroy its effectiveness. In other words, in order for the system to work, it had to be followed to the letter. Once you started to add your own ingredients, you started to upset the fine balance upon which the system was developed.

For example, one small element of the Weight Watchers system is that participants are asked to record their daily food intake in detail. Now you might wonder what record keeping has to do with weight loss. However, there was an amazingly high degree of correlation between weight loss and those who kept accurate records! Those who followed the system and recorded their food intake lost weight. Those who did not follow the system and did not record their food intake seemed to never lose weight.

The only way I can account for this observation is that we all report to a higher authority. In the area of weight loss, we can call that higher authority the "Great God of the Scale." Unfortunately, the Great God of the Scale is always watching, even when you are not recording your food intake. As such, I am certain that those who did not lose weight did not keep accurate records of their food intake. However, the Great God of the Scale did keep accurate records and made certain that they did not lose weight at the end of the week. The key point is that the Weight Watchers system includes record keeping. If you want the system to work for you, accurate record keeping must be part of the program. There can be no compromise.

Just like there is a Great God of the Scale, there is also a Great God of the Sale who watches your prospecting and selling activity. Follow the rules set forth by the Great God of the Sale, and your results will be very predictable: You will be a selling superstar. Violate those rules, and you proceed at your own risk. The 10 Commandments of Prospecting is a proven success formula for prospecting and selling success.

COMMANDMENT 1: Make an appointment with yourself for one hour each day to prospect.

Prospecting requires discipline. Prospecting can always be put off until a later day when the circumstances will be better. I can assure you that the time will never be exactly right to prospect. Make an appointment each day to prospect. Prospecting should be placed on the same priority level as a meeting with a client or potential client or a meeting with your boss. Write the appointment into your time management system, and do it! Prospecting is so important to me that I even do it on my cell phone, usually when driving my car. I do use a hands-free kit as required by law. This practice can be very productive for me. This is often the only time I have to myself during the day. Although some might consider this practice extravagant, if I make one additional appointment each month I believe that I receive a very generous return on my investment.

COMMANDMENT 2: Make as many calls as possible.

Smart Prospecting taught us only to call the best prospects in the market. Therefore, every call we make has the potential to be a quality call, since we are calling only those prospects who are most likely to buy large quantities of our product or service. Make as many calls as possible during the hour. Since every call is a quality call, more is always preferred to less.

I've often been asked whether I take calls during my prospecting hour. The answer is a resounding "No!" While prospecting, my phone is always on DND (Do Not Disturb), and my door is always closed. If you set aside one hour a day for prospecting, make certain that you make one full hour of calls. Any distractions will serve only to dilute your efforts. Remember, the Great God of the Sale is always watching and will reward you only on the basis of the Law of Sowing and Reaping, not on the Law of Intending to Sow.

COMMANDMENT 3: Make your calls brief.

The objective of the prospecting call is to get the appointment, unless you are in telesales. I will talk about telesales in a moment.

You cannot sell a complex product or service over the phone, and you certainly don't want to get into a debate of some sort. Your prospecting call should last approximately two to three minutes and should be focused on introducing yourself and your product, briefly understanding the prospects' needs so that you can provide them with a very good reason to spend some of their valuable time with you, and, most important, getting the appointment.

If you reflect on the strategy outlined in the previous chapter, you should see that your job as a professional salesperson is to find those prospects who are ready, willing, and able to buy now, as fast as possible, while repositioning the remaining prospects in your target market to an appropriate spot in your sales pipeline. Given that you are trying to find those prospects who are ready to buy now, as fast as possible, a rejection at this point in the sales cycle should be viewed as a positive event in that it allows you to reposition the current prospect to a later point in your sales pipeline, while now moving on to other prospects who might bear more immediate fruit. This is not to imply that you do not want to make a bona fide attempt at getting an appointment with your current prospect but rather to suggest that you don't want to expend undue effort in doing so. When you really think about it, if a prospect is not ready, willing, and able to buy now, there is very little you can do to change this situation. Therefore, you need to know this as soon as possible so that you can move on to those prospects with a need for your product or service and make your investments there.

With respect to telesales, your goal is also to get an appointment. It is the same type of appointment that you will get in field sales with the exception that your meeting will be held over the phone. The purpose of your initial meeting, whether in field sales or in telesales, is to "discover" the customer's or prospect's needs. I call this a "discovery session."

At a discovery session, you ask the prospect or customer a series of open-ended questions (a question that cannot be answered with a brief response) to learn about or discover his needs. A discovery session is an information-gathering session.

I said earlier that if you are in field sales, your goal is to get an appointment. This means that at the end of your prospecting call you might say something like, "Great! I am going to be in your area next

Tuesday and would like to stop by and introduce myself. Are you available at 3:00?"

If you are in telesales, you might say, "Great! What I would like to do is ask you a few more questions now to see if I can help you in the area of. . . ."

In both field sales and telesales, the goal of the prospecting call is actually to enter discovery. The only difference is that in field sales, the discovery session typically takes place on a later day at the customer's office, while in telesales, the discovery session often takes place as the second stage of the call.

In telesales, you can also set up discovery sessions for a later date just as you would in field sales; however, your discovery session will still take place on the phone, not in the prospect's office.

We are going to discuss scripting in depth in the next chapter of this book.

COMMANDMENT 4: Be prepared with a list of names before you call.

Again, the Great God of the Sale is always watching. Not being prepared with a list of names will force you to devote much, if not all, of your prospecting hour to finding the names you need.

If you recall, we talked about market intelligence resources in Chapter 5. There, we referred you to Hoovers, OneSource, Factiva, Harte-Hanks (for technology companies), Google, and the company Web site. In Chapter 5, I also gave you a 10-step process to develop your account list or contact list. This is one of the most important set of activities you can do as a professional salesperson.

I acknowledge that this will take time but, remember, I likened this to an investment. In any business, you must make an upfront investment of capital in order to get the business started. Sales is (unfortunately) no different. Defining your account, prospect, and contact list is your upfront investment. The way it works is that you make this initial investment to start the prospecting, territory, or account development process, and then you make ongoing investments, much smaller in magnitude, to keep refining your contact list over time.

Also remember that you will always be busy, you will always feel as though you are working hard, but if you are not prepared with a full, complete, and prioritized contact list, you may jeopardize your calling time. Research time is not calling time.

At a minimum, you should have at least a one-month supply of names on hand at all times. However, this is a bare minimum. I fully recommend that you follow the 10-step process outlined in Smart Prospecting so that list management will never be an issue for you.

As an aside, I have found that trading for leads can be a very effective supplemental way to build a prospect database. This is a supplement to purchasing the names from highly qualified sources like those we discussed earlier and in our discussion of Smart Prospecting. Remember, all salespeople are in the same boat. We are all in need of leads in order to survive.

It has been said many times in the past that time is money. Leads are money, too! In fact, they're the lifeblood of your career and should be treated with due respect. In order to trade leads, find someone in a complementary business who is likely to call upon the same types of prospects that you are, and trade.

In my case, I was in the computer training business. I traded leads most often with sales representatives from software publishers. We both sought to find technology decision makers and influencers in large corporations. Companies that sold training, other than computer training, would also be good trade candidates for me.

A second recommendation that will probably surprise many of you is to consider trading lists with your competitors. Although this might sound surprising, there is no more qualified list around other than your own, so why not trade?

After you have gotten over the shock of this recommendation, please consider the facts. First, I have found that there are no secrets as to who the decision makers in a company are. If you can find them, so can your competitor. If this is the case, why not develop a qualified list as soon as possible? By trading lists with your competitor, you will have substantially increased your effectiveness. Of course, both you and your competitor could have found every decision maker in the marketplace by yourselves. But this takes time. Trading lists will allow you to accomplish your goal of covering the market quite a bit faster than had you attempted to do it yourself.

Second, if you are not doing a good job servicing your customers, your competitors will wean them from you over time. If you are doing the best you can to service your customers, you will have nothing to worry about by having your competitor call on your leads. Finally, if your competitor cannot convert a lead, why not give you the opportunity? This action will stimulate demand in the industry and give your competitor (or you, if the tables are turned) a better shot next time around.

Earlier, I stated that trading leads is one of the best ways to develop a qualified list other than through purchased lists. When I refer to purchased lists, I want to distinguish between the type of list you would buy for direct-mail purposes and the type you would buy for telephone prospecting.

Lists purchased for direct-mail purposes typically have better prospects than those that you could quickly garner from your local business publication, a company Web site, the public library, or your local Chamber of Commerce. A direct-mail list will have names of prospects who have at least expressed an interest in your type of product or service or a closely related product or service. In contrast, contacts on lists taken from local business publications and other similar sources may not have expressed any interest in what you are selling.

Recall our earlier discussion about purchased information and free information. Lists taken from your local business publication, for example, have a nominal cost (they are essentially free), and, as a result, you must spend a great deal of your own time to survey the list and find those prospects who might have an interest in your wares.

However, there are typically lists that are even better than those used for direct-mail purposes. These are lists that are highly qualified by the seller, typically through phone interviews and other techniques. In other words, the seller of the list has spent a great deal of time finding exactly who might have a strong interest in your product or service. This is time that you would otherwise have to spend yourself, which is why the sellers of the list can charge a premium for the prospects they provide to you. These lists can often provide you with multiple decision makers per company location and multiple company locations. Some lists go as far as to provide you with information on your prospects' strategic direction in the industry. These are the purchased lists that will yield your greatest return on investment. The data sources that we have discussed in this book—Hoovers, OneSource, Harte-Hanks, and Factiva—all fall into this category.

COMMANDMENT 5: Work without interruption.

I recommend that you not take calls and not entertain meetings during your prospecting time. Take full advantage of the prospecting learning curve. As with any repetitive task, the more often you repeat the task during a contiguous block of time, the better you become. Prospecting is no exception to the rule. Your second call will be better than your first, your third better than your second, and so on. In sports, this practice is called getting in the groove. You will find that your prospecting technique actually improves over the course of your prospecting hour.

COMMANDMENT 6: Consider prospecting during off-peak hours instead of during conventional prospecting times.

At first, this idea may seem trivial, but I can assure you this is a high-impact recommendation.

One day, I was driving to a client for a presentation. It was about 8:00 in the morning. The presentation was to start at about 9:00. The drive to the client was nice and easy. I was near my home and was driving on a major highway. The highway was straight, and there wasn't much traffic, so I decided to make a few calls.

Before I arrived at the client, I was able to make 10 calls. Eight of the 10 calls were actually completed. This is amazing. In this day and age, with the prevalence of voice mail, getting a direct contact with the person you want to speak to is very hard. I don't think you need me to tell you that. Yet, I was able to complete eight of the 10 calls that I made. Remember that a completed call is one where you call the prospect and actually speak with the person you intended to. The outcome of the conversation is not relevant at this point. As long as you speak to the person you intended to, I consider the call completed. We will talk more about some benchmarks that you can use to measure your progress when we talk about reporting and tracking, in the final chapter of this book.

The next day, I was driving to the same client but another location. The drive was much longer so I was able to make 20 calls instead of 10. On this day, I was making the calls between 9:00 and 11:00. I made 20 calls and left 20 messages. I did not get even one completed call.

So why was I successful on the first day and not on the second day? I am the same person, I was calling from the same list, I was just as enthusiastic, and everything else was the same. Everything except for one thing: the time that I was calling. On the first day I was using nonconventional prospecting hours, and on the second day I was calling during conventional prospecting hours. The time of the day at which you make your calls can have a major impact on your success.

What I am about to tell you relates to prospecting in the United States. Workdays and the best times to call vary by region of the world. My experience has shown me that prospecting during lunch works well in the United States but will not work well at all in Latin America. In Latin America, they take very long, traditional lunches. My experience has shown me that prospecting bright and early in the morning is very important in the United States; however, in India, the workday gets off to a slower start that I am used to in the United States, and prospecting in the morning may not bear as much fruit.

So, there are better times to prospect and less productive times to prospect. Unfortunately, these highly productive times vary by region and even by individual. As you know, some of us are morning people (like me), and some of us are evening people.

If you are a morning person, prospecting from 8:00 to 9:00 in the United States should be very productive. However, if you are an evening person, you may want to prospect from 5:00 to 6:30, as this is a great time to prospect and your energy levels will be high.

I'm sure you know if you are a morning person, a day person, or an evening person. Please take your biological clock into account when you are planning your prospecting time. Beyond your biological clock, you must learn when the best times to prospect are in your country. The way to figure this out is very simple.

When you start prospecting after reading this book, simply create a grid of the day. Segment the grid by hours: 8:00 to 9:00, 9:00 to 10:00, and so on. Do this all the way up to 6:30 P.M. (or 18:30 for those of you who use a 24-hour clock). On the first day, make at least 10 calls in the first hour; 8:00 to 9:00. On the second day, make at least 10 calls in the second hour; 9:00 to 10:00. Continue this process each day until you reach 6:30. Then, repeat the process.

You will have cycled through the hours in the day twice at this point. If you did not skip any hours in the day (I recommend that you try out each hour without prejudice at this point), you will have gone through each of the 10 hours in the work day two times. In other words, you will have tested the 10 hourly segments in the day two times each. Having made at least 10 calls in each hour, you will have made 20 calls per hourly segment, or 200 calls in total.

When I am suggesting that you make a call, all I am asking you to do is to press the requisite buttons on the phone until the phone rings. Once the phone rings, you have made a call, irrespective of the outcome of the call. What I want you to do is record both your calls (dials) and your completed calls (success in speaking to the person you intended to). Please note that completed calls include your direct completed calls (you called the prospect and she picked up the phone) and your completed callbacks (you called the prospect and left a message, and the person called back and reached you). When the prospect calls back, a completed call counts only when you speak with the prospect. If the prospect did not reach you directly and left you a voice mail instead, the call does not count as a completed call.

So, you will have tracked both your outbound dials and your com-

pleted calls over about one month. Calculate the ratio of dials to completed calls and you will see the top times to call. I recommend that
you focus very heavily on the top three times you noted in your test.
Member, if you follow this recommendation, your productivity can be
as high as 80 percent. If you do not follow this recommendation, your
productivity can be as low as zero. That's quite a contrast.

In the United States, conventional cold calling hours are between
9:00 A.M. and 5:00 P.M. What I am recommending is that you set
aside one hour each day to prospect. The best times to prospect (in the
United States) are between 8:00 A.M. and 9:00 A.M., between noon
and 2:00 P.M., and between 5:00 P.M. and 6:30 P.M. You can always
supplement your prospecting times with times during the day other
than these. However, these times generally bear the most fruit.

As I mentioned, you need to determine the best prospecting times
for you. The best times will be a function of where you live, what
industry you are in, and how you work. I am just trying to illustrate,
by example, what works best for me.

As an additional observation, I have found that truly successful
people, and truly successful salespeople, do not work from 9:00 to
5:00. Rather, these hours allow you to break even. You must put in
that extra effort in order to be successful.

I am not suggesting that you become a workaholic. Rather, I would
always prefer to see you work smart as opposed to hard. Mark Mc-
Cormack, the chairman of International Management Group, in his
book *The 110 Percent Solution*, says that hard work must be part of the
equation.

You will find decision makers, go-getters like yourself, often work
during off-peak hours. You will find that their assistants, those who
often separate you from the person you are trying to reach, may not
work during these hours. Take full advantage of these unguarded moments. But also take heed. When you call, be prepared to talk. The
idea of calling during off-peak hours works with an extremely high
degree of effectiveness. I have seen too many occasions where the
salesperson dialed the phone, reached the person she dialed, and was
unable to speak—this, after months of trying to reach the decision
maker during conventional hours.

In addition to increasing your cold-calling effectiveness, cold calling at off-peak hours will earn you the respect of those you are trying to reach. To me, the most crucial element of a sale is not what happens prior to the sale but what happens after the sale.

Think about going out to buy a car. Would you prefer that the salesperson give you a box of candy prior to the sale to earn your business or would you prefer that she be there after the sale to support this very expensive purchase? I would prefer the latter.

Calling prospects during unconventional calling hours sends a clear message to the prospect. It says that you are dedicated to your work, your company, and your product. It says that you are the type of person who is going to go that extra mile to see that your customers get the return on their investment that they anticipated when they made the purchase.

I recommend calling during the hours determined earlier as a primary prospecting strategy. Calling during other hours should be used as a fallback strategy when, for whatever reason, you cannot not make your prospecting calls during the times that you calculated as the best for you.

Special tip for Commandment 6: I have found one minute in particular to be unusually fruitful. This is 11:59. I'm not certain why this time has been so good for me—perhaps it is psychological; perhaps it is because companies are in transition at this time. Nonetheless, save this secret for your best prospects as 11:59 will present you with a maximum of 250 golden opportunities per year! Also, as long as you are already prospecting, don't put down the phone. Consider moving on and prospecting from noon to 1:00 P.M. It will pay big dividends, especially after you read Commandment 9.

COMMANDMENT 7: Vary your call times.

We are all creatures of habit. So are your prospects. In all likelihood, they are attending the same meeting each Monday at 10:00 A.M. If you cannot get through at this time, learn from your lack of success, and call this particular prospect at other times during the day or on other days. You'll be amazed at the results. If you are wondering just how you might track your calls, let alone your call times, read Command-ment 8.

COMMANDMENT 8: Be organized.

I use a popular contact management system called ACT! I have used it for many years. I strongly suggest that you use a contact manage-ment or CRM system, as well. The contact management or CRM sys-tem you choose should allow you to record a follow-up call three years from tomorrow with no more difficulty than it would be to record one for tomorrow.

Here lies another great secret of prospecting. If a prospect tells you to call back in three years, six months, ten days, and five hours because his contract expires with his existing vendor on that date, do it! Nothing should fall through the cracks. Further, and possibly more important, because you can record your follow-up activity in such great detail, there should be no emotion associated with a "no." When a prospect tells you the time is not right, you can simply schedule him for follow-up at a later date. As they say in the computer industry, it's as easy as 1-2-3.

The advantages of a contact management system are many. First, if you follow the recommendations outlined in this book, you are going to make a large number of prospecting calls. If you are like me, you may not remember the nature of every callback you get. You might be asking yourself, "Who is this person, and why is she calling me?" If she is in your prospecting database, you will have your answer. She is returning your call. A contact management system gives you the ability to easily access your contact records.

Second, a contact management system allows you to keep detailed records on each of your prospects. In addition to the basics of name, address, and phone number, you can keep detailed records of call ac-tivity, call times, and even detailed call information. This information facilitates not only your initial call but also call follow-ups by making it quite easy to generate electronic correspondence and e-mails.

While I know that people were selling long before there were computers (my mother told me this), computers and other technology certainly facilitate the sales and prospecting process. The key here is to be organized whether or not you use a contact management system, though I hope that there are none of us left out there that have not adopted technology. Remember, the one who keeps the best notes wins.

COMMANDMENT 9: Envision the end before you begin.

Stephen Covey, in his book *The Seven Habits of Highly Effective People*, tells us to see the end before we begin. Dr. Covey is, in effect, telling us to establish a goal and then develop a plan to work toward that goal. This sage advice works well in prospecting and new business development. Your goal is to get the appointment, and your plan—your cold-call script—should be designed to achieve your goal.

Dr. Covey's recommendation, coupled with a healthy dose of confidence, will do much to enhance your chances of making a successful cold call. I recommend that you use visualization techniques to enhance your level of confidence. Prospecting is fraught with rejection and sometimes even less-than-polite prospects. Much of this book, so far, has been devoted to teaching you how to overcome the anxiety associated with these negative influences. We now introduce one more idea to help you overcome the anxiety associated with rejection: confidence. Confidence will go a long way in overcoming the fear of rejection.

Before you begin each call, see the prospect eagerly awaiting your call and desperately in need of your services. You call to introduce yourself and the prospect responds, "Where have you been all my life?!" You schedule the appointment. In other words, see your success before you make each call to ensure that both your confidence and enthusiasm are at peak levels.

This approach has two major benefits. First, it will help move you toward Rejection-Proof Prospecting, a goal that we set earlier in this book. Remember, we should all believe that our product or service will make the customer better off. Your role is simply to spread the good word about your offering. Confidence will enhance your ability to do so and will allow you to make more calls.

Second, your confidence and enthusiasm will be contagious. After all, if you were the person on the other end of the phone, who would you be more likely to buy from: someone who is confident and feels strongly about his product or service or someone who is unsure of himself? I believe the answer is obvious.

COMMANDMENT 10: Don't stop at the close of the sale.

Persistence and follow through are key virtues in selling success. In my book *Red-Hot Customers, How to Get Them, How to Keep Them,* one of the topics reviewed is the six ways to add value to your customer's business. The six ways to add value are business know-how, supply-chain optimization, operational support, ease of doing business, organizational strength, and product/service design.

One of the six ways to add value to your product or service is through the stability of your organization. In other words, if you are buying a complex (and expensive) product or service from an organization, is it of value to you that the organization survive for the life of the product in order to honor its warranty and service the equipment? The answer is again an obvious "yes."

Customers value not only stability in the organization but also stability in the salesperson. The salesperson must be available after the sale to support the product or service. It is the salesperson, hand in hand with the customer, who develops the value-added recommendations that help the customer enhance her profitability. There is a great deal of teamwork involved in an effort to optimize the value of your product in the client's organization. Further, without the expertise of the salesperson, it is not clear that the value-added strategies and recommendations will come to full fruition. Customers want to know that you will be there to help them implement the recommendations that you made.

The challenge is that you must have a way to demonstrate stability prior to a sale. The answer lies in persistence. Although I do not recommend calling a particular prospect once a day, I do strongly recommend following the call and visit goals outlined in Chapter 5. We discussed setting call goals of, say, once per month for high-priority accounts.

This plan should be tempered with a subjective assessment of the next appropriate time to call back. For example, if the prospect is on the verge of making a major decision, I would clearly call back more frequently. On the other hand, if the prospect has just signed a major two-year contract with one of your competitors, you may want to consider calling back less frequently.

The key here is that you must call back. You can never lose a sale until you decide to quit. If you are persistent, while constantly trying to earn the right to advance, you will notice a change of attitude among your customers and prospects. They will begin to admire your persistence. They will understand that you are a force in the industry and a player to be reckoned with. You will get the appointment.

I have often read that most sales are made after the fifth call and most salespeople quit after the first. In order to keep my persistence at its peak, I reflect upon a very powerful story that I once read about persistence. This story would be enough to keep even the most complacent of us motivated to make the next call. The story is "Three Feet from Gold," from Napoleon Hill's classic, *Think and Grow Rich*. Briefly, the story is as follows:

There was a man who left home to search for a gold mine. He went into the hills and discovered a very rich vein of ore. He had the gold analyzed to confirm his discovery, and, sure enough, he had unearthed one of the purest veins of gold ever discovered. The man returned home to tell his friends and relatives so that he could borrow the necessary funds to cultivate the mine. He raised the necessary capital and returned to the mine to cultivate his fortune.

The gold began to flow as easily as water, and soon the man had recouped approximately half of his original investment. Then, without warning, the vein ended. The man dug furiously but could not recapture the vein. Finally, he gave up, sold the mine and mining equipment to a junk dealer for scrap, and returned home, broke and a failure.

Before scrapping the equipment, the junk dealer decided to hire a mining expert to study the mine. The expert, upon a detailed survey of the land, revealed that the vein had not dried up but rather shifted three feet to the left because of a fault in the earth. He advised that if the junk dealer were to continue digging in the new direction, he would soon recapture the vein and become fabulously wealthy.

The junk dealer acted on the advice of his mining expert, went on to retap the vein of ore, and became one of the richest people in the United States. Meanwhile, the original miner had to live the remainder of his days with the knowledge that he stopped "just three feet short of the gold."

How would you like to live with a similar feeling? Your next call, whether it be the fifth one to the same person over time or the thirtieth call of the day, could be the one that recaptures your vein of ore. Do you want to take the chance that you'll stop and someone else will collect the gold that really should have been yours? I certainly don't! Also, remember that most sales take place after the fifth call. Most salespeople stop after the first. Your persistence will pay off. It has to. This is the Law of Sowing and Reaping.

I would like to share an idea that has worked extremely well for me as a supplement to my persistence. Salespeople should have their own personal stationery for use with customers and prospects. Handwritten, hand-addressed, and hand-stamped notes and envelopes can do much to enhance the probability of success in the sales cycle by differentiating both you and your company, as well as by demonstrating stability. While reading an industry publication or a general business publication, always be on the watch for information and articles about your customers and prospects. When you find a positive article, clip it out and send it to your customer, along with a congratulatory handwritten note. This practice will raise your visibility among your customers and prospects.

A Reminder

To reiterate, the 10 Commandments are:

Commandment 1: Make an appointment with yourself for one hour each day to prospect.

Commandment 2: Make as many calls as possible.

Commandment 3: Make your calls brief.

Commandment 4: Be prepared with a list of names before you call.

Commandment 5: Work without interruption.

Commandment 6: Consider prospecting during off-peak hours if conventional prospecting times don't work.

Commandment 7: Vary your call times.

Commandment 8: Be organized.

Commandment 9: See the end before you begin.

Commandment 10: Don't stop.

CHAPTER 7

Anatomy of a Cold Call

When I review the 10 Commandments of Prospecting, one thing becomes readily apparent: We need an 11th commandment! The 11th commandment should be practice, practice, and practice some more. Harvey Mackay, the noted author and public speaker, has an interesting saying: "Practice does not make perfect; perfect practice makes perfect." Whether practice or perfect practice makes perfect, one thing is very clear. In order to be effective at prospecting, you must practice.

All professionals practice. Skaters practice for years before a performance in the Olympics. Professional athletes practice day in and day out for their actual performances on the athletic field. Why should professional salespeople be any different?

The question is, practice what?

I recommend that you practice your cold calls. After all, does it make sense to learn on the job? Your reputation and success are at stake.

Develop a Script

The first step in practicing your cold calls is to develop a script. The value of a cold-calling script is severalfold.

First, a script will ensure that you are prepared. In addition to professional considerations, being prepared will allow you to be in control of the call. If you are in control of the call, you will be much more at ease, since you will control the flow and direction of the conversation.

The second benefit of being prepared is consistency. Once you develop something that works, stick with it. A script will allow you to do that. I don't mean to imply that, once the script is written, you should never again reevaluate it. What I do mean to say is that there are core elements to a script. This chapter will teach you what they are. Although you should stick with the script that works for you, like a public speaker, always reevaluate your script to make it better. Never make major modifications to your script. Introduce small changes to your script, when appropriate, and test your changes in low-exposure environments.

All of us have received cold calls both in the office and at home during the evenings. The calls can come from a variety of sources. The common thread of many of these calls is that it is clear the person on the other end of the phone is reading from a script. This type of cold call has done little to enhance the image of the professional salesperson. Believe it or not, the only thing that separates these types of calls from the truly professional calls is a little bit of practice.

For many years, I was a member of Toastmasters International. It is at my local Toastmasters Club that I heard some of the best speeches of my life. I always asked the speakers the key to their success. Without exception, they all said "practice." The typical Toastmaster practices more than one month to deliver a speech of five to seven minutes. Investments in your script will help you become proficient, conversational, and relaxed. These skills will certainly increase your probability of success in the selling process.

I would venture to say that if I made 10,000 cold calls, each call would be identical in both form and substance. This may sound like quite a statement, but it's really not. I have dissected my cold call, put it back together, practiced it thousands of times, and fine-tuned it over numerous years of experience. An experienced veteran of corporate sales in our organization claims to make the same call each and every time she sits down to prospect.

I would like to present you with my cold-calling script and then analyze its basic elements so that you can develop one of your own. Please notice that I am not asking you to use my script or the one used successfully by our sales veteran for more than 40 years. Rather, I am asking you to learn from what we have done and then develop a script that suits your personality.

It would be very difficult for you to take a script that suits my nature and present it as naturally as I do. Rather, you must develop one that works for you, using the basic elements of a cold call as your guiding light. My prospecting script is presented in Figure 7-1.

I have studied public speaking for a number of years now, and one of the greatest assets of a speaker is to sound conversational. This is very difficult to achieve and devastating to those speakers who cannot achieve it. The same could be said with equal emphasis of prospecting. Your cold-call script must sound conversational in order to be effective. We have all received calls from someone who is obviously reading from a script. I'm sure we all have had the same reaction—to get off the phone as quickly as possible. Only a simple script can be conversational.

Let's take a few moments to analyze the elements of my script. While the words will change from person to person, the elements should remain constant. Once you find the perfect script for you, you'll never change and you'll never look back!

FIGURE 7-1 Basic cold-calling script.

Mr. Jones, please. Hello, Mr. Jones. This is Paul Goldner of Sampson Management Company. How are you today? Great! We have not spoken before, but we have been working with companies in your industry for many years. One of the chief concerns we are hearing from others in your position is the need to improve the effectiveness of their management information systems. Is this the same issue impacting your business, or are there other ones? [Mr. Jones responds.] Great! We have been very successful in helping companies like yours overcome issues very similar to these. I'm going to be in your area on June 25 and would like to stop by and introduce myself. Are you available at 3:00?

Get the Prospect's Attention

The first element of a successful cold-call script is to get the attention of the prospect. Remember, he was not waiting for your call and was probably thinking about another subject when you called. Your first job is to break the prospect's preoccupation with what he was doing so that he pays attention to you. You have seconds to accomplish this goal.

The easiest way to get someone's attention is to state his or her name. Dale Carnegie, in his best-selling book *How to Win Friends and Influence People*, states that "A person's name is to that person the sweetest and most important sound in any language." Further, current studies indicate that people think about themselves 95 percent of the time. So, to get the prospect's attention, I use the following statement:

Mr. Jones, please. Hello, Mr. Jones.

Not leaving anything to chance, I use the person's name twice in my opening statement. Further, please feel free to use the person's first name if this feels better for you. When people ask for Mr. Goldner, my first instinct is to look for my father.

Introduce Yourself

The second element of a successful cold-call script is to introduce yourself. You should be quite accomplished with this and can consider the following statement:

This is Paul Goldner of Sampson Management Company. How are you today? Great!

Introducing yourself is an integral part of this statement. However, what really makes the statement work is the phrase "How are you today?" Remember, you are making a cold call, and the prospect knows this. There is a natural barrier between the prospect and yourself. What you need at this point is what professional speakers call an "ice breaker"—a phrase or statement delivered by the speaker to draw the audience into the speech. In this case, the ice breaker is designed to draw the prospect into your conversation. The phrase "How are you today?" works just great here. Interestingly enough, I almost never get a negative response to the question "How are you today?" The typical response I receive is either positive or neutral, at worst. This question also borrows from another of Dale Carnegie's strategies: to "[become] a good listener, [he] encourages others to talk about themselves." This advice is great not only for cold calling but also for face-to-face selling. Obviously, it is also a key element in interpersonal relations.

It's at this point in our script development process that I must tell you an interesting story. In all of my seminars, I always receive negative comments about the question "How are you today?" Please keep in mind that I have never received a negative response to this question, so years of experience tells me that it is okay to ask this question.

When I travel to Europe to deliver my "Red-Hot Cold Call Selling" seminars, I even get more resistance to the question "How are you today?" than I do in the United States. I have been told that in Europe, people that you do not know will not appreciate your asking how they are.

For years, I had no other alternative but to listen to my friends, colleagues, and students in Europe. However, recently, I found myself in Copenhagen delivering a prospecting seminar to workers at a major company in Denmark.

The first part of the day was devoted to education. I gave a prospecting seminar, and someone from the company taught about a new product that we were going to try to set up meetings for during the second part of the day.

After the training, we developed our scripts and were actually going to start making some calls. Unfortunately, everyone was afraid to make the calls, so it was up to me, the instructor, to show them how easy it was.

I wanted them to see that we had developed a good script, that we had practiced the script, and that even I could make a cold call in a foreign land and with limited product knowledge.

So, using my cell phone, I employed the techniques of Smart Prospecting taught in Chapter 5 of this book. My first cold call in Denmark in the history of my selling career was to the largest prospect in the company's target market.

Just so you know, in Europe, cell phones are commonly used for business-to-business communications. It is quite acceptable to prospect on your cell phone. The reason that I point this out to you is that I prospect on my cell phone all of the time. However, here in the United States, people who attend my programs are very wary about using the cell phone for prospecting and new-business-development purposes.

I see nothing wrong with it, and I think that it is interesting to note that our European colleagues are also quite comfortable prospecting by cell phone. I urge you to consider this "best practice" as it will greatly enhance your sales productivity. Remember, as long as you are honest, legal, ethical, and polite, anything else is okay in the world of professional sales.

So, getting back to our story, I picked up my cell phone and prepared to make my first cold call in Denmark. I have to admit that my Danish is very rusty, so I decided to make the call in English, my native language. Since I have made hundreds of thousands of cold calls, cold calling for me is nothing more than a reflex. I call as easily as I breathe.

So, I went into reflex mode and began to make the call, using essentially the script presented in Figure 7-1. The script was obviously tailored to the circumstances of the company I was working with, but, other than that, it was unchanged.

There were about 75 people in the program, and all of them had their eyes riveted on me. Not one of them was able to make a call, and here I was, a stranger to their country, making cold calls to their top prospects. The room was dead silent as everyone waited to hear what I was about to say.

Can you guess what I said?

Of course you can! I said, "Mr. Jones, please, hello, Mr. Jones. This is Paul Goldner of XYZ Company. How are you today?"

When I said "How are you today," just about everyone in the room let out a large gasp. This poor man from the United States was about to get yelled at by the company's top prospect. After all, you don't ever say "How are you today?" in Europe unless you already know the person. I had been told not to say "How are you today?" but, unfortunately, I was operating on reflex. I could not help myself.

So, I said it, and what do you think happened?

I shouldn't tell you, but I will. The prospect said, "Fine, how are you?"

The members of the class couldn't believe what they had just heard. However, I do not tell you this story to prove that I was right and they were wrong. I tell you this story to illustrate several points.

First, prospects are not as unfriendly and unreasonable as one might think. In fact, in all of my years in prospecting, I have met very few unfriendly people on the telephone. Also, I want you to understand the value of professionalism. Prospects know how to differentiate between a professional and a nonprofessional. I was professional, and so there was nothing wrong with what I did.

Third, and most important, was there is no right or wrong way to prospect. I did it my way, and someone else may do it differently. You can say "How are you today?" or you can ask another question, a trivial question, at this point in your script.

The question that you ask is, quite frankly, not very important. What is crucial to your success is that you ask a question.

If you do not ask a question at this point, you sound unprofessional, because you are talking at the prospect and the prospect will know this. The key at this point in your script is to get the prospect engaged in the call, and you can do this only by getting the person to talk. Asking a question is the way you get the other person to talk in a sales conversation.

Since you are at the beginning of your script, you can not ask a very sophisticated question. However, you can ask a trivial question like "How are you today?" If you do not like this question, develop another one for you to use. However, at this point in your script, *you must ask a question*. A question, at this point, will separate the successful calls from the unsuccessful calls.

Once I listen to the prospect's response, I always respond with an emphatic "Great!" Great is one of my favorite words. It has been said that selling is the transfer of enthusiasm about your product or service to the prospect. Once prospects become as enthusiastic about your offer as you are, you have made a sale. I start the transfer of enthusiasm from the point of first contact with the prospect. "Great" starts the transfer process.

There is a second key element built into this aspect of our cold-call script. The "old school" of selling taught the salesperson to be a great presenter. The "new school" of selling teaches the salesperson to be a consultant. An effective consultant must listen to and understand the prospect's or customer's need. This requires the ability to ask effective questions.

I like to start the consultative sales process during the cold call by asking two questions in my script. The first question is "How are you today?" As noted, this question, albeit a simple one, establishes the framework for the consultative sales process.

State Your Reason for Calling

This is the third element in a successful cold-call script. Consider this statement:

> We have not spoken before, but we have been working with companies in your industry for many years. One of the chief concerns we are hearing from others in your position is the need to improve the effectiveness of their management information systems.

There are many keys to a successful prospecting script, and the reason for your call is one of them. Let's see why.

The first sentence of your reason for the call is fairly obvious: "*We have not spoken before.*" You are probably stating this because, first, it is true, and second, it is a very polite way to get the conversation started with the prospect.

Continuing on with the first sentence, it says, "*but we have been working with companies in your industry for many years.*" There is a lot of significance in this portion of the sentence.

I believe that the single biggest impediment to a sale is the customer himself: "If I purchase this product or service from you, will it work?" In other words, customers are always asking themselves this question: If they proceed with the transaction or relationship, will the transaction or relationship be successful?

If the answer to the question is no, they will probably buy from the competition. If the answer to the question is yes, then I believe that the prospect will likely buy from you.

If you consider a normal purchase or sales transaction, it tends to work as follows. First, you give the money to the vendor, then the vendor gives you the product or service, and finally, you get to see whether the product or service did what it was intended to do.

For example, if you buy a car, you must pay for the car first. Then, you get to drive the car home. Only after you have driven the car for several months do you get to see if you have made a wise purchase decision.

Likewise, you attend a sales training seminar. You must pay for the seminar in order to gain admittance. You attend the seminar and probably like what you heard, but it is only after several months of implementing what you have heard that you get to see if the seminar was worthwhile.

While I agree that there are instances where the purchase or sale transaction may not exactly follow the pattern that I have outlined, I do believe that you need to be adept at answering the question "If I buy from you, will it work?"

What you are doing with the statement *"but we have been working with companies in your industry for many years"* is actually using a very powerful selling tool, that of a third-party reference.

A third-party reference is one that uses someone outside your company to answer the question "If I buy from you, will it work?" The reason this is such a powerful technique is that you are providing third-party evidence about the likely success of the relationship.

In this particular instance, you are providing general evidence by stating that you have worked in the industry for many years. The implication is that if you had done a poor job along the way, you probably wouldn't have lasted in the industry for as long as you did. This is a very important statement to make because it both provides you with credibility in the cold-call process and starts to answer the question, "If I buy from you, will it work?"

There is a second type of reference that it pays to discuss at this point, and that is a more specific reference, or what I call an application reference. An application reference is a reference story done for a particular company about a particular thing (application) that you successfully completed within that company.

An application reference more definitively responds to the question, "If I buy from you, will it work?" It is a good idea, if you are going to prospect, to have an application reference handy. I'm certain that most customers will want to answer the question "If I buy from you, will it work?" before they meet with you. After all, if you are not going to provide a quality solution to them, why would they want to spend some of their valuable time with you? They wouldn't.

So, when you are on the phone, it is likely that customers will test you and your credibility before they agree to meet with you. An application reference is the best way to respond.

While you do not want to have a detailed discussion with the customer if you are a field sales professional trying to get an appointment to better understand the prospect's needs, you do have to be responsive to the prospect's questions. If she asks you whether you have worked in her industry before or whether you have successfully completed the type of application you are proposing to her in your prospecting message, you need to be prepared.

A statement such as "For example, one of the recent projects we successfully completed included the successful implementation of an application very similar to yours," will go along way to getting you the appointment.

If there is one thing that I have learned over the years, it is to be prepared. There are several things you can always count on arising in various stages of the sales process. The first is that the customer will always question the price of your product or service (the "price" objection). The second is that when you are prospecting, the customer will usually tell you that she is working with the competition (the "competitive" objection). And, finally, she will always ask you, "If I buy from you, will it work?" (the "will it work" objection).

We will talk more about objections in Chapter 9, but suffice it to say that we know that these three objections will come up in every sales cycle. If you know that they are coming, why let these objections take you by surprise? There is no need for that, especially if you are a professional.

I do want to quickly address the telesales aspect of reference stories, as well. Earlier, I said that when you are prospecting, you do not want to get into a lengthy discussion on the telephone. This is clearly true of field sales, when the objective of the prospecting call is to get the appointment. In telesales, however, the objective of the call is to enter the discovery process.

While the telesales discovery process is the same as the field sales discovery process (both are a series of structured, open-ended questions designed to learn about the customer's needs), the processes take place in different venues.

In field sales, the discovery process usually takes place at the customer's place of business. In telesales, the discovery process often takes place on the phone immediately after the cold-call segment of your script. So, when I said that a prospecting call should be fairly brief, I was referring to field sales only. In telesales, it would be great if you could extend your prospecting call into the discovery phase of the sales cycle.

In either event, whether you are in field sales or in telesales, please be prepared with a reference story to be certain that you can respond to the "will it work" objection.

The second sentence of the "State Your Reason for the Call" segment of your basic prospecting scripts is extremely important to your prospecting success. A statement such as *"One of the chief concerns we are hearing from others in your position is the need to improve the effectiveness of their management information systems"* is what I would call a business-oriented prospecting script.

It is crucial that you have a business orientation to every prospecting script that you develop. In contrast, a nonbusiness-oriented script may read as follows: *"The reason I am calling is that I am the new account executive assigned to your account and I would like to stop by and introduce myself."* As you will see when you continue with this book, a statement like this is flawed in many ways.

First, it does not differentiate you from the competition. The next time you are talking with your prospect or customer, ask him how many cold calls he receives in a day or a week. I'm sure that he receives calls from all of your competitors, and I'm sure that he receives calls from myriad other vendors with whom he works or who would like to do business with him. Every (nonprofessional) prospector in the world uses the "introduce myself" script. Trust me, if you leave a message like this, the prospect will not even remember that you called.

Second, a script or statement along these lines give you little to work with when you need to call the prospect a second time because the first time you did not get the appointment (because of the script that you used).

Finally, in working with our clients, I have proven, at least to myself, that this script does not yield the appointments you require. I have gone as far as to set up a control group using the "introduce myself" script and compared the results to those of a second group using a business-oriented script. They results were definitive. I have seen instances where the control group did not get even one appointment, while the group that used the business-oriented script got a "fair" proportion of appointments. Just so you know, we will address how many appointments you should get when you are cold calling in Chapter 13.

So, it is important that you have a strong business orientation to your prospecting call. This should be built into your reason for the call. As important, it will set you up to go on to the next segment of your script.

Ask a Question

By making a statement such as *"One of the chief concerns we are hearing from others in your position is the need to improve the effectiveness of their management information systems,"* you are going a long way to support your prospecting success.

We discussed the need to have a strong business orientation to your prospecting call. The reason this is so important is that it will differentiate you from the competition and set you up to achieve your objective for the call.

The way to have a strong business orientation to the call is to consider the industry or company that you are calling into. If you study the industry or the company (using the market intelligence resources discussed in Chapter 5), you should be able to identify a potential business issue within the industry or at the company.

I say "potential business issue" because you have not made the call yet. Prior to making a call on a prospect, you can only surmise what might be a potential business issue. You can never be certain.

Because you can never be certain you must ask the following (great) question:

Is this the same issue affecting your business, or are there others?

This is one of the best questions I have ever heard. A positive or a negative answer to this question should set you up for an appointment.

If the prospect says, "Yes, this is the issue impacting our business," you can explain to the prospect that you have been very successful at helping other companies overcome this concern.

If this is not the issue that is impacting the prospect's business, then the person should be compelled to tell you the challenge the company is in fact facing. Again, you can respond in the same way, explaining that you have been very successful in helping other companies overcome this concern. Have examples ready.

In either case, you should be setting yourself up for the appointment that you started out to get.

Consultative salespeople are at their best when they are asking probing, open-ended questions. The salesperson does very little talking and a lot of listening. By asking the foregoing open-ended question, I give the prospect a great deal of latitude in telling me about his business and its needs. The big benefit to me is that, because of the latitude I have given the prospect, he will, in all likelihood, give me the opportunity to identify a need of his company and thus establish the basis for a face-to-face appointment.

Most books on this topic that I have read recommend that you make a strong benefits statement at this point. A statement like the following is often suggested: "Mr. Jones, I'm sure that you, like many of my best customers, would like to save several thousand dollars on the cost of. . . ."

To me, this approach does not sound at all professional. I'm not aware of anyone who would not like to save several thousand dollars. It's a silly question, and the prospect might be offended that you asked it.

Further, it is my strong belief that people will buy from you if you offer them an appropriate return on their investment. You can do this only if you first understand their business and their needs. Ultimately, the prospects must draw their own conclusion that they want to meet with you or buy your product or service. Your job is simply to help them along to reach this conclusion. Listen carefully, and without interruption, to their response.

Get the Appointment

Now you go for the close.

You have just listened attentively to the major challenge this prospect is currently facing. At this point in your script, I recommend that you do two things.

First, I like to rekindle the transfer of additional enthusiasm from me to the prospect. I believe that this will help you get the appointment.

I would start out my response by saying *"Great!"* (Please note that your response of "Great" is in reference to the prospect's comments about the current business challenge the company is facing. Again, the main reason that this word is included in my cold-call script is that it helps you to build enthusiasm for your product and to sound confident in your position as a valuable resource for the prospect.)

Once I have rekindled the enthusiasm transfer process, I then call up the power of third-party references again by saying that we have helped other companies in their industry with similar business issues. Please note that in your basic script, it is not necessary to provide a reference story at this point. However, you may be asked to by the prospect, so it is a good idea to have a reference story or two available every time you pick up the telephone.

Now that I have transferred additional enthusiasm for our potential meeting and now that I have reused the power of third-party references, I go for the close. In the case of field sales, the close is your
effort to gain your appointment. In telesales, the close is you effort to
enter the discovery process. One way to close in field sales is by saying,
*"I'm going to be in your area on June 25 and would like to stop by and
introduce myself. Are you available at 3:00?"* The analogous statement
in telesales would be, *"What I would like to do is ask you a few more
questions now to see if we can help you overcome the challenges you are
currently facing."*

There are several important points here. First, before each call,
decide when it will be most convenient for you to meet with the prospect. My schedule is always set up to maximize my productivity, not
the prospect's. Although this philosophy may sound like it doesn't
serve the needs of the prospect, remember that the name of the game
is to maximize your return on the time you invest in the sales process.
You should be flexible, but still keep in mind that you need to be as
efficient as possible.

I recommend having an exact date and time to offer prospects.
This date and time should be selected prior to your phone call and
should be the one that best suits your busy schedule. I find that offering prospects only one time changes the focus of the discussion to
when they will meet with you. Offering alternative times, as recommended in other prospecting texts, leads the discussion to whether the
prospect will meet with you, not when. Remember, it is crucial that
you get the appointment. When you select Smart Prospecting as your
priority-setting mechanism, every appointment that you get is a good
one, because every prospect lies clearly within your target market.

A second important strategy is to have a second time that you can
meet that will also suit your schedule. The reason this is important is
that it is very likely that the prospect will not be able to meet you at the
first time you suggest. So, before I pick up the phone, I actually plan
two times to meet: the best time for me and the second best time for
me. I make two bona fide attempts at trying to get the meeting on my
terms.

If I cannot get the meeting on my terms, I say (after making the two attempts), *"Is there a time and date that works best for you?"* This will allow me to get the appointment, though not at a maximally convenient time.

A good schedule of appointments would be a meeting at 8:00 A.M. and then one every two hours thereafter. Over the years, I have found that a one-hour appointment is a good, solid meeting, and you can typically get from one end of any city in the United States to the other in the additional hour with time to spare. Your administrative duties, such as letter writing, proposal writing, and updating your database, should be handled early in the morning, late in the evening, and on the weekends. Your prospecting and selling time is unfortunately limited to conventional business hours. In most businesses, you can't see a prospect on a Sunday afternoon or call one at 9:00 P.M. Because prospecting and selling time are limited by conventions outside your control, I recommend maximizing your prospecting efforts during the time allotted.

Review the Cold-Call Script

A summary of the key elements of a cold-call script follows:

1. Get the prospect's attention.
2. Introduce yourself.
3. State your reason for calling.
4. Ask a question.
5. Get the appointment.

Your job is to build a simple, conversational script that best reflects your sales personality.

Now that you understand the fundamental elements of a cold-call script, it may be a good time to acknowledge that you don't always get the appointment. Therefore, you need a cold-call and business-development process or strategy that will ensure that you will get sufficient appointments to satisfy your sales goals and increase your market penetration. This strategy is the subject of Chapter 8.

However, before moving on, I would like to introduce your Cold-Calling Tool Kit: a collection of items that you should have with you when you do your prospecting. These items are all designed to give you that extra competitive edge that we first discussed in Chapter 1.

Your Cold-Calling Tool Kit

Some of the items in your Cold-Calling Tool Kit may appear a little unusual at first. In fact, when I review the kit at my seminars, I always hear people whispering the same question: "I wonder if he really does that stuff?" Well, the answer is, "Yes I do!" and so will you once you see how helpful these suggestions will be.

The first element in your Cold-Calling Tool Kit is a mirror. Yes, a mirror. When making a cold call, it is imperative that you sound as good as you can over the telephone. The importance of how you sound on the phone cannot be overemphasized. You have exactly two minutes to convince a complete stranger to make an appointment with you. Even worse, the second you begin to speak, your prospects immediately begin to form a mental image of what they think about you. What do you want their mental image to be? It's up to you, and the mirror will help.

You should place your mirror directly in front of you and make certain that your hair is well groomed, that your clothes are neat and orderly, and that you sit up straight in your chair. This appearance check will make you sound powerful over the phone and help you to project confidence and conviction. When prospecting, you should never undo your tie, roll up your sleeves, slump in your chair, or put your feet up on the desk. All of these items will lessen the quality of your verbal image on the phone. I have a tendency to slump in my chair when I'm tired. One look in the mirror picks me right up. I continue with my calls and, more important, I project an image of power, confidence, and conviction.

I'm sure that you always try to look your best in your face-to-face selling opportunities. You would never dream of attending a business meeting looking disheveled, because your appearance would likely disqualify you from the sales competition. Likewise, you should never sound disheveled over the phone. I have seen many salespeople over the years who look impeccable in person but sound disheveled over the phone. This greatly limits their opportunities in the sales world.

For those of you who might feel self-conscious with a mirror on your desk, I have found one for my desk that looks like a picture frame. From my side of the desk, it is a mirror. From the other side of the desk, it looks like the back of a picture frame.

The second tool in the kit is a tape recorder. For less than $100, you can have a tape recorder hooked up to your telephone handset. Taping yourself allows you to answer the question: "If I were a prospect, would I give myself an appointment?" You may find the answer to this question very difficult to confront at first. However, it is important to know how you look and sound to others if you are to project the best possible sales image. When you speak, you hear yourself through the vibrations of the bones in your head. When you listen to yourself on a tape recorder, you hear ourselves as others do, through your ears. The difference is profound.

Further, we all have little speech idiosyncrasies that we could do without. The most common of these are the "ahs" and "ums" that we use to fill up the time between thoughts and sentences. They can be very distracting and should be eliminated from your speech patterns.

As I noted earlier, I am a member of Toastmasters International, a public-speaking club that I recommend to those who want to improve their communication skills. At each Toastmasters meeting, one designated club member counts the "ahs" and "ums" in the speeches— a very effective technique for helping a speaker to eliminate these useless space fillers.

We all know how funny we look and sound to ourselves when we see ourselves on TV or hear ourselves on tape. All of us have much room for improvement. Your tape recorder will be a nice addition to your personal development program.

A third tool is a telephone headset. Telephone headsets are another relatively inexpensive addition to your existing phone system. The headset frees your hands for taking orders, working on a computer, taking notes, and dialing the phone faster. All professional telemarketing groups make use of these devices. Further, headsets give you freedom to move about your office. It is not uncommon to have the prospect ask a question that requires you to look up the answer in a book or on the Internet.

With a headset, you can continue the conversation, walk over to your bookshelf, or type on your computer, and retrieve the information you are looking for without having the prospect know that you even moved.

A second benefit of a headset is that it allows you to stand when you speak on the phone. If you have ever watched a really great public speaker, you know that, most likely, the speaker was standing, not sitting. There are several reasons for this. The obvious one is that the speaker needs to be seen. The less obvious one is that the speaker can be more animated in a standing position. She can better use hand gestures and project her voice while standing. If selling success is in any way defined by the transfer of enthusiasm about your product or service from you to the prospect, then telephone headsets give you much greater freedom to stand as you prospect and help you project enthusiasm for your product or service with great emotion.

Fourth, consider the use of a call-timing device, especially if you have a tendency to make your prospecting calls last more than two to three minutes. You do not need anything elaborate to time your calls. A three-minute hourglass will tell you if you are spending too much time on your prospecting calls. Remember, the purpose of your call is to get an appointment (or enter discover for telesales). Two to three minutes should be sufficient in most instances to allow you to accomplish your goal.

Fifth, never forget your trusty script. While I'm certain that you will eventually internalize your script, and that using it will be as natural as speaking your own name, it pays to have it around in the heat of battle. Sometimes, even the best of us lose our train of thought, particularly when working during very stressful periods or if we don't have a private office. A handy script will allow you to quickly collect your thoughts and resume the pursuit of your goal: the appointment.

CHAPTER 8

Your Prospecting and Business-Development Strategy

Before I lay out our prospecting and business development strategy, it is important to understand the foundation upon which it is developed. The strategy we are about to unveil is based on three fundamental premises: the Law of Sowing and Reaping (Chapter 2), the Selling Life-Cycle Paradigm (Chapter 4), and consultative selling (my *Red-Hot Customers* book), in that you will always be providing your prospects with new and valuable information.

In addition to these fundamental laws of professional selling, you must also understand that there are really only three potential outcomes to any given call: either you speak to the person you were trying to reach and get the appointment, you speak to the person you were trying to reach and don't get the appointment, or you don't reach the person you are targeting. These outcomes are presented graphically in Figure 8-1.

Getting the Appointment

Clearly, the first possibility—speaking to the person you were trying to reach and getting the appointment—is the easiest and the preferred outcome. Your basic script, detailed in Chapter 7, will work quite well

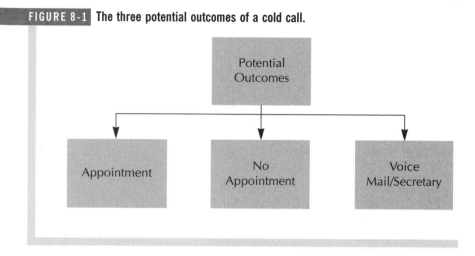

FIGURE 8-1 The three potential outcomes of a cold call.

here. In summary, you reach the person you were targeting and get the appointment.

In this instance, a confirmation e-mail or letter sent on the day or the day after you make the appointment would be a nice supplement to your call, and calling a day in advance to confirm the appointment would also be a good idea.

A sample confirmation e-mail has been included in Figure 8-2 for your reference.

Sending a confirmation e-mail is extremely professional and will do a lot to enhance your position in the eyes of the prospect; so will calling a day in advance to confirm the appointment.

This latter point is a hotly debated topic in the world of professional selling. Your options are not to call to confirm your appointment, to call a day in advance to confirm your appointment (as I recommend) or to call the day of the appointment to confirm your appointment.

Those who support the first position—not calling to confirm—argue that the prospect is then given an opportunity to cancel the appointment. Although this is true, I think the prospect has that option with or without our calling. The prospect can either call you to cancel, or if the prospect had something unexpected come up, may simply not be available when you arrive.

FIGURE 8-2 **Sample confirmation letter.**

June 2, 20XX

Mr. Robert Jones
Director of Administration
NYT International
15 South Salem Avenue
Lower Newton Falls, MA 06000

Dear Mr. Jones:

It was a pleasure to speak with you today [yesterday]. I look forward to our meeting on Wednesday, June 25, 20XX, at 10:00.

I will call the day before to confirm the appointment. In the interim, should you require any information or if I can be of assistance, please do not hesitate to call.

Yours very truly,

Susan Simms
Account Manager

[Note: For an e-mail, you would leave out the formal heading or address. You might even want to address the person by his or her first name if this is the custom in your country.]

Therefore, I suggest calling to confirm either the day before the appointment (the preferred method) or the day of the appointment. Either option works.

If you call a day in advance and the prospect cancels the appointment, you have more time to react and salvage the hour or two that you planned for the meeting. Canceled appointments give you a great opportunity to do additional prospecting.

What Next?

This first part of our business development strategy is depicted in Figure 8-3. In summary, you call the person you were targeting and get

FIGURE 8-3 Business-Development Strategy—Part One.

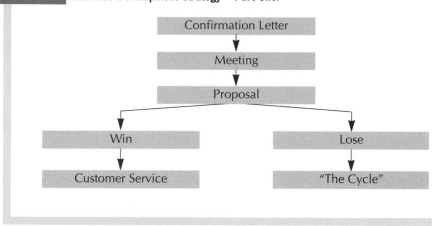

an appointment. You use your basic script to do this. Once you get the appointment, you send a confirmation e-mail (Figure 8-2). You also call one day in advance of your appointment to confirm.

Ultimately, you will go on a meeting, develop a proposal for the prospect, and either win or lose a sale. Please note that a proposal need not be a lengthy document as is often associated with the work proposal. A proposal can be a lengthy proposal document outlining your solution to the customer, but it can also be something as simple as a verbal concept or offer on your part so that the prospect has something to buy. I am just trying to illustrate that you are at a crucial decision-making point in the sales cycle.

Assuming that you win, your job is to provide superior customer service. However, what do you do if you lose the sale? This is where most salespeople stop the business-development process. In *REDHOTSALES*™, we are just beginning!

Losing a Sale: What's Next?

If you reflect back to the discussion of Smart Prospecting in Chapter 5, we went to great lengths to define our target market. Our definition was based on one or more objective demographic factors. Losing a sale does not change the demographics of the prospect account. Even though we lost the sale, we must place the prospect back in our sales pipeline and continue to work with the prospect in some manner. This is exactly the point we were making when we first introduced you to the Selling Life-Cycle Paradigm, as well.

A "no" today simply means that you place the prospect back into the sales pipeline for continued cultivation. The question that comes to mind is this: What do you do to further cultivate the account? After all, you just lost a sale!

After you lose a sale, I recommend that you place your prospect into the "Business-Development Cycle" (Figure 8-4). The Business-Development Cycle may be one of the most powerful tools you have available as professional salespeople. You will use this tool to recultivate lost sales, to overcome objections, and even to overcome voice mail. The cornerstone of the Business-Development Cycle is your company's Unique Selling Points.

Over the years, I have taught tens of thousands of sales professionals how to sell. I have worked with companies of all sizes, in many (or most) industries, and have been to every major market in the world. One interesting observation that I have made during this time is that every company has its strengths relative to the competition.

The key to making the Business-Development Cycle work for you is to have a good command of your company's strengths, or what I call your company's Unique Selling Points. Your company's Unique

FIGURE 8-4 The business-development cycle.

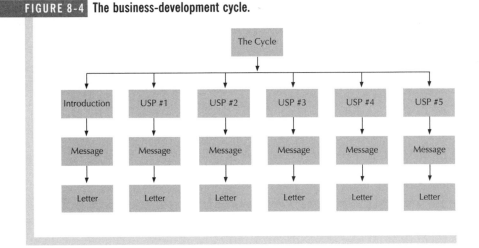

Selling Points should be your company's five greatest strengths in the market. They should be extremely customer focused (i.e., each point should be meaningful in the minds of your customers and prospects), and they should differentiate your company from the competition. Remember that if your Unique Selling Points ("USPs") do not truly differentiate you from the competition, customers will make this a major issue in your sales cycle with them.

In order to illustrate how the Business-Development Cycle works, let us assume that you work for Office Tech, Inc. Office Tech is a global organization that manufactures high-technology computer systems and software to improve the productivity and time to market for their customers. The Unique Selling Points and the related customer benefits are outlined in this section. Please note that because we are using a fictitious company for purposes of our illustration, we will assume that our USPs do differentiate us from the competition. Without a real-life comparison or case study, there would be no other way to illustrate our points of differentiation.

[First-to-market commitment] Office Tech is consistently first to market with new products. This allows Office Tech customers to stay on the cutting edge of technology and enhance their products and services prior to their competition.

[Local field service support] Because Office Tech is a global organization, it provides its customers with local field service support for all installed systems. The big benefit to Office Tech customers is minimized downtime for all installed applications.

[Global organization] As noted, Office Tech is a global organization. The company is able to support other multinational corporations with a consistent solution worldwide and a single point of contact for all service and technical support issues.

[Broad product line] Office Tech sports the broadest product line in the industry, providing high-technology business solutions along all stages of the price/performance spectrum. Office Tech serves as a single-source solution to its customers.

[Research and development testing facility] Office Tech not only supports the largest research and development budget in the industry but also allows customers and prospects to test potential solutions in its own testing facility with no incremental charge to the customer.

I encourage you to spend a few moments outlining your company's unique selling points. Figure 8-5 has been provided for your convenience. Your Unique Selling Points are going to be critical factors in your selling success and will be used throughout the remainder of this book. Accordingly, you should become intimately familiar with them. In fact, you should be able to recite them in your sleep, and they should permeate each and every sales conversation and presentation that you make.

There is one additional point that I would like to make before we examine the Business-Development Cycle in depth.

There are certain companies that I have worked with that have

FIGURE 8-5 Form for compiling your company's Unique Selling Points.

Unique Selling Points
for

_____

Office Tech Incorporated	Your Company
Global Organization	
First-to-Market Commitment	
Local Field Service Support	
Broad Product Line	
R&D Testing Facility	

incredibly complex business structures, incredibly complex products, and incredibly complex product lines. If your company is one of those companies, you may have to make a small adjustment to the Unique Selling Point strategy discussed here.

Most companies can do just fine with only five Unique Selling Points. However, if you are General Electric, for example, and have more than 10 distinct business units at the top level of your organization, you may first think that you need five Unique Selling Points for each major business unit. Likewise, if you are IBM, with three major businesses (servers, software, and services), with very broad product lines in each business, or if you are Applied Materials, with incredibly complex products and product lines, you again may believe that you need more than five Unique Selling Points. First, keep in mind that these subsets of companies are all part of one larger organization (GE, IBM, Applied Materials). On the basis of this viewpoint and because your Unique Selling Points are supposed to be the company's guiding light from a sales and marketing perspective, I would suggest that five Unique Selling Points would still be all that's necessary.

However, having worked in these environments for many years, I know that some of you reading the book will disagree. I would encourage you to really think this through, but I will also compromise and suggest that three of your five Unique Selling Points should be corporate and inviolate. I will allow two Unique Selling Points to cover the unique situations you think you may have in your business.

What I have seen over the years is that companies will start with my compromise position (three corporate Unique Selling Points and two specific Unique Selling Points). However, over time, as they thing about what they are doing and begin to apply the Unique Selling Points to their business, they usually migrate to the five corporate Unique Selling Points that I recommended initially.

So, let's get back to the Business-Development Cycle. The Business-Development Cycle allows you to continue to work with a prospect, even though you just lost a sale. The reason is that each time you call the prospect, you are providing her with new (and valuable) information. In other words, you are giving the prospect a new reason to call you back, a new reason to meet with you, and a new reason to buy from you. Second, you are prepared each and every time that you call. Let's see how to use the Business-Development Cycle to overcome your lost sale.

Assume that you just lost a sale to a top priority prospect. On the basis of the parameters we outlined in Chapter 5, you would be required to call the prospect once a month (if it was a top-priority prospect), *even after the lost sale*. The issue then becomes what you should say. Here's where your Unique Selling Points come in.

The reason I believe that you may have lost the sale is that you may not have been as effective as necessary in tying the needs of your prospect to one or more of your strengths or Unique Selling Points. If you recall, we defined selling as an education process, and here is where the education comes to bear in a very significant way.

There is another really interesting point here. When I deliver my seminars on this topic (prospecting and new-business development), I always get asked, "How can I call the prospect back right away after I just lost the sale?" The answer to this question is obvious.

Let's say that today you lost a sale to a top-priority prospect. According to the call cadence presented in Chapter 5, you would be required to call the prospect whose opportunity you just lost (the prospect selected your toughest competitor).

If you have been in sales for any significant period of time (say, more than three years), you should notice that companies and individuals buy again and again. So, if your customer just bought your product or service from the competition, you know that it is going to buy a similar product or service three months, six months, one year, or even further down the road. The key here is that it will buy again!

So, if you lose the original sale (and feel rejected) and decide not to call back ever again, you set your destiny in stone. You will never again do business with this particular prospect. However, if you use my approach, that of calling back periodically, you will start to increase your chances of winning a future sale.

I am not in a position to guarantee that my approach will work, but I can tell you that the other approach, that of giving up, will not work. So, I will leave it up to you to choose your prospecting destiny.

Now, let's see how I would apply this approach.

Let's say that I just lost a sale to a high-priority prospect. The call cadence established in Smart Prospecting would recommend that I call the prospect back on a monthly basis. In reality, I may wait one quarter, to let the prospect get started with the new vendor, and then call back to see how the relationship is working out. Remember, not all new relationships work out well.

After my first call back, I would return to the standard call cadence and my Unique Selling Points scripts, which we are going to develop later.

For moderate-priority prospects, I would wait for one half-year before my first call (instead of one quarter), and for lower-priority prospects, I would call according to the original cadence, since we are calling these companies only twice a year, anyway. Then, I would return to the normal call cadence for each of these two categories of accounts.

What we are going to do is develop a series of scripts and letters or e-mails around each of our Unique Selling Points. In this way, you will always have something new and interesting to present to your prospects. In other words, you will be giving them a new reason to return your call if you are facing voice mail, a new reason to meet with you if you are having difficulty getting an appointment, and a new reason to buy if you are not making a sale.

Assuming that you just lost a sale, the next time you speak with a prospect, you may want to have your message focus on the first of your five Unique Selling Points. A sample script, using the first of the unique selling points of Office Tech, is outlined in Figure 8-6.

As you review Figure 8-6, I want to call several things to your attention.

First, take a look at the script in Figure 8-6 and compare it to the script in Figure 7-1. What has changed (excluding the name of the salesperson, which I changed just to keep the book interesting)? Not much! In fact, the only thing that changed is "the reason for your call."

This is a significant point for you. All you need to do is to take create a Unique Selling Point script from your basic script is to change

FIGURE 8-6 **Sample script for a call focusing on your first Unique Selling Point (first-to-market commitment).**

Mr. Jones, please. Hello, Mr. Jones. This is Susan Simms of Office Tech. How are you today? Great! One of the chief concerns we are hearing from others in your position is the need to have their office systems keep pace with their business needs and the needs of their customers. Is this the same issue impacting your business, or are there other ones? [Mr. Jones responds.] Great! We have been very successful in helping companies like yours overcome issues very similar to these. I'm going to be in your area on June 25 and would like to stop by and introduce myself. Are you available at 3:00?

your reason for the call. This makes it very easy and time-efficient to create your Unique Selling Point scripts (assuming that you created a good basic script).

Second, please take the time to notice how we position our first Unique Selling Point (First-to-Market Commitment). We positioned it with a question, "Is this the same issue impacting your business, or are there others?" Remember, selling is all about asking questions and listening to your customer. Talking about your company, your product, or yourself at this point in the sales process will only diminish your credibility.

Finally, please take a moment to consider that the entire focus of the script is on the customer. Other than telling the customer who you are and what company you work for, there is very little mention of you. All too often, when I see people prospecting, they use a script that tells the customer as much as they can about their company and product (as fast as they can) in the hope that they might say something interesting and grab the prospect's attention. This is clearly an approach that I do not agree with.

Assuming that you get the appointment (with your first Unique Selling Point script), your standard confirmation e-mail will work just fine (Figure 8-2). However, assuming that you don't get the appointment, a follow-up e-mail (or letter) reaffirming your first-to-market commitment would be very appropriate. A sample follow-up e-mail has been provided in Figure 8-7.

FIGURE 8-7   **Sample follow-up letter focusing on your first Unique Selling Point (first-to-market commitment).**

September 15, 20XX

Mr. Robert Jones
Director of Administration
NYT International
15 South Salem Avenue
Lower Newton Falls, MA 06000

Dear Mr. Jones:

It was a pleasure to speak with you today. I'm sorry that we were not able to get together. However, I did want to provide you with an example of how our first-to-market commitment can help your business be more successful.

As you know, Office Tech recently introduced a new, high-technology office system that will revolutionize the way companies do business. This system has been shown to reduce total cost of ownership by as much as 20 percent in companies like yours. Given the size of your organization and your commitment to provide state-of-the-art products to your customers, I thought this new system might be of value to you. We are seeing a strong need for this type of solution among our largest corporate accounts.

I have enclosed some information on our new solution for your review, and I will be contacting you shortly to discuss your interest in this idea. In the interim, should you require additional information or have any questions, please do not hesitate to contact me.

Yours very truly,

Susan Simms
Account Manager

[Note: For an e-mail, you would leave out the formal heading or address. You might even want to address the person by his or her first name if this is the custom in your country.]

Again, assuming that you didn't get the appointment by using your First-to-Market Commitment Unique Selling Point script, you need to start to think about what your next step is going to be. Remember that we took the time to rigorously define our target market in Chapter 5. Smart Prospecting told us that every company on our prospect list, and every call that we make, is a quality prospect and a quality call. Just because we did not get the appointment on our first or second try does not mean that we can stop trying.

To stop calling an account within your target market will do nothing more than to diminish your prospects as a salesperson, and we certainly don't want you to do that.

So, because you cannot drop the prospect from your account list, you must figure out a way to approach the person again, and again, and again. This is where the power of your Unique Selling Points and your Business-Development Strategy come into play.

Because you have five Unique Selling Points and a basic script, you have six different ideas that you can position at your customer or prospect in order to get the appointment. If you consider that the difference between your basic script and your Unique Selling Point scripts is simply one sentence (by providing a new reason for the call), you should now realize the power of what we have accomplished.

We have just provided you with six valid reasons for the call.

All too often, when I observe people trying to prospect, I see that they struggle with a reason for the call. In fact, I have heard people say that they would be happy to call if they just had a good reason. I have also seen entire organizations paralyzed by the fact that they did not have a good reason for the call. Last, I have seen sellers spend untold amounts of time in between calls just thinking of something good to say to the next prospect.

All of these issues can easily be solved by simply having a great basic script (Figure 7-1), a great set of Unique Selling Points, and a great set of Unique Selling Point scripts.

So, assuming that you didn't get the appointment by using your first-to-market strategy (first Unique Selling Point script), you would be required to call the prospect again. The interval, and this is also very important to you, will be determined by the category of prospect in your Smart Prospecting analysis (Chapter 5) and the call cadence you established in Smart Prospecting, as well.

If you recall, in Chapter 5, we segmented our target market into three categories of prospects; high, moderate, and low (but still quality accounts). We set call goals for each category of prospect; once a month for high-priority prospects, once a quarter for moderate-priority prospects and once a half-year for lower-priority prospects.

While these are only sample call goals and you need to establish your own call cadence, you can see that you will have to call your prospects time and time again according to the cadence. They reason that you have to make the multiple calls is that it will take multiple calls for you to get your first sales appointment.

So, if you have used your first Unique Selling Point script and the prospect either didn't agree to a meeting or did return the voice mail that you left, it is my opinion that when you call back (according to your call cadence), you must change your message. This is a very important point for us as sales professionals.

It is my opinion that if you leave a strong, business-oriented message of the type advocated in this chapter and the prospect does not call you back, this means that the prospect was not interested in the Unique Selling Point that you positioned. While the Unique Selling Point is a valid point to position, it may or may not be relevant to any given prospect. Understanding what is relevant to any given prospect is part of the prospecting process, and rotating through your Unique Selling Point scripts is a great way to figure this out.

So, if your first Unique Selling Point script did not work, the you must move on to your second Unique Selling Point script. Using our sample company, you would focus on local field service support instead of the first-to-market commitment. A sample script and follow-up e-mail have been provided for your reference in Figures 8-8 and 8-9.

Again, assuming that you do not get the appointment using your second Unique Selling Point script, you would move on to your third Unique Selling Point, then your fourth, and then your fifth. Sample scripts and follow-up e-mails have been provided in Figures 8-10 through 8-15.

The strategy we are outlining here teaches you an effective way to penetrate accounts. Many salespeople enter a new selling situation

FIGURE 8-8 Sample script focusing on your second Unique Selling Point (local field service support).

Mr. Jones, please. Hello, Mr. Jones. This is Susan Simms of Office Tech. How are you today? Great! One of the chief concerns we are hearing from others in your position is the need to have next-day parts and service on all of their technology systems. Is this the same issue impacting your business, or are there other ones? [Mr. Jones responds.] Great! We have been very successful in helping companies like yours overcome issues very similar to these. I'm going to be in your area on June 25 and would like to stop by and introduce myself. Are you available at 3:00?

expecting to become the exclusive provider of goods or services for the target company immediately. This is akin to saying to the prospect: "Hello. You don't know me. Would you please give me all of your business?"

If someone were to ask this question of you, how would you react?

Let's review what I am talking about in more depth (see Figure 8-16).

All prospects have two types of needs: core needs and niche needs. Core needs are defined as that set of prospect needs that is readily available in the open marketplace. It is something that you can easily provide to the prospect, and it is something that your competitors can easily provide as well.

Core needs are typically filled by your standard products and/or services. Core needs represent that largest portion of the customer's needs or available business, and they are the target that all salespeople typically aim for.

Niche business, on the other hand, is that portion of a customer's needs that is not readily available in the open market. This is because the need is either not readily identified or not readily available in the market. A niche need is something that you or your company is (you hope) uniquely qualified to fill.

If the niche need is not readily identified, the prospect is typically unaware of the need, and, most often, it can be revealed only through skillful questioning on the part of the salesperson. In the case where

FIGURE 8-9 Sample follow-up letter focusing on your second Unique Selling Point (local field service support).

September 15, 20XX

Mr. Robert Jones
Director of Administration
NYT International
15 South Salem Avenue
Lower Newton Falls, MA 06000

Dear Mr. Jones:

It was a pleasure to speak with you today. I'm sorry that we were not able to get together. However, I did want to provide you with an example of how our local field service support can help your business be more successful.

As you know, Office Tech has warehouses and technicians in most major markets around the world. Given the need to minimize downtime in most companies, I thought the ability to receive next-day parts and service might be of value to you. We are seeing a strong need for this type of service among our largest corporate accounts.

I have enclosed some information on our local field service support solution for your review, and I will be contacting you shortly to discuss your interest in this idea. In the interim, should you require additional information or have any questions, please do not hesitate to contact me.

Yours very truly,

Susan Simms
Account Manager

[Note: For an e-mail, you would leave out the formal heading or address. You might even want to address the person by his or her first name if this is the custom in your country.]

FIGURE 8-10 Sample script focusing on your third Unique Selling Point (global organization).

Mr. Jones, please. Hello, Mr. Jones. This is Susan Simms of Office Tech. How are you today? Great! One of the chief concerns we are hearing from others in your position is the need to have a single point of contact for all of their technology and technical support needs. Is this the same issue impacting your business, or are there other ones? [Mr. Jones responds.] Great! We have been very successful in helping companies like yours overcome issues very similar to these. I'm going to be in your area on June 25 and would like to stop by and introduce myself. Are you available at 3:00?

the niche opportunity is not readily serviced, the prospect is aware of the need but has yet to find a qualified source of supply.

The problem with setting your sights on only the core needs of the prospect is that the prospect likely has already identified the need for what you do and has found a provider for the product or service. Further, if the current provider is not doing an adequate job, the prospect has likely replaced it with a provider that will. In other words, it is unlikely that you will walk in off the street and be able to easily able to fill the core needs of your prospects. This may happen, but it's more likely the result of luck than a well-planned strategy.

As an alternative, I would like to suggest that you develop a strategy around niche opportunities. These niche opportunities should be based on your Unique Selling Points. Keeping in mind that prospects likely have fulfilled their needs for the core business opportunity, you must continuously search for new and innovative ways to help them achieve their goals. If you simply offer the "status quo," why should a prospect take time out of her already busy day to meet with you?

Presenting new and innovative ways to improve a prospect's profitability will help you win those smaller sales that come from the prospect's niche opportunities and your Unique Selling Points. This will give you the opportunity to prove your capabilities. Once you have done this, you can then move to additional smaller sales, and ultimately, larger sales. As you continue to move through the account

FIGURE 8-11 **Sample follow-up letter focusing on your third Unique Selling Point (global organization).**

September 15, 20XX

Mr. Robert Jones
Director of Administration
NYT International
15 South Salem Avenue
Lower Newton Falls, MA 06000

Dear Mr. Jones:

It was a pleasure to speak with you today. I'm sorry that we were not able to get together. However, I did want to provide you with an example of how our global technical support capabilities can help your business be more successful.

As you know, Office Tech offers our customers a single point of submission for all technical support issues worldwide. This capability has helped our customers speed up their time to market by as much as 30 percent in companies like yours. Given the size of your organization and every company's need to service its customer base, I thought this capability might be of value to you. We are seeing a strong need for this type of solution among our largest corporate accounts.

I have enclosed some information on this solution for your review, and I will be contacting you shortly to discuss your interest in this idea. In the interim, should you require additional information or have any questions, please do not hesitate to contact me.

Yours very truly,

Susan Simms
Account Manager

[Note: For an e-mail, you would leave out the formal heading or address. You may even want to address the person by his or her first name if this is the custom in your country].

| FIGURE 8-12 | Sample script focusing on your fourth Unique Selling Point (broad product line). |

Mr. Jones, please. Hello, Mr. Jones. This is Susan Simms of Office Tech. How are you today? Great! One of the chief concerns we are hearing from others in your position is the need to have the ability to leverage technology at any point along the price/performance spectrum. Is this the same issue impacting your business, or are there other ones? [Mr. Jones responds.] Great! We have been very successful in helping companies like yours overcome issues very similar to these. I'm going to be in your area on June 25 and would like to stop by and introduce myself. Are you available at 3:00?

development cycle, you will have also developed a tactical strategy that allows you to surround the core business opportunity.

At this point, it becomes appropriate to discuss the core needs with your customer.

If you reflect back on what we covered in Chapter 5, you should remember that we recommended that you call your high-priority accounts once a month, your moderate-priority accounts once a quarter, and your lower-priority accounts once every half-year. Following this type of a callback strategy and combining it with the Unique Selling Point messages outlined in this chapter, you should see that our business-development process gives you half a year's worth of messages if you are calling a high-priority account, 18 months' worth of messages if you are calling a moderate-priority account, and three years' worth of messages if you are calling a lower-priority account. In other words, you always have something new and important to say to your prospects.

Further, this system can be reused.

When you get to the end of your Unique Selling Point messages, you simply start over. You can start by reintroducing your company to the prospect. After all, quite a bit of time has passed since you first used an introductory message. Further, when you get to your Unique Selling Point messages, you should present them with a slightly different angle. In other words, you should be delivering a series of new and improved messages.

FIGURE 8-13 **Sample follow-up letter focusing on your fourth Unique Selling Point (broad product line).**

September 15, 20XX

Mr. Robert Jones
Director of Administration
NYT International
15 South Salem Avenue
Lower Newton Falls, MA 06000

Dear Mr. Jones:

It was a pleasure to speak with you today. I'm sorry that we were not able to get together. However, I did want to provide you with an example of how our end-to-end product portfolio can help your business be more successful.

As you know, Office Tech has the broadest portfolio of technology solutions on the market. This allows our customers to buy the capacity they need today (and only the capacity that they need today), yet have a clear growth and technology road map for their future business needs. Given the size of your organization and the need for all companies to purchase cost-effective solutions that yield a strong return on their investment, I thought our solution portfolio might be of value to you. We are seeing a strong need for solution options in the market.

I have enclosed some information on our total-solution portfolio for your review, and I will be contacting you shortly to discuss your interest in this idea. In the interim, should you require additional information or have any questions, please do not hesitate to contact me.

Yours very truly,

Susan Simms
Account Manager

[Note: For an e-mail, you would leave out the formal heading or address. You might even want to address the person by his or her first name if this is the custom in your country.]

FIGURE 8-14 Sample script focusing on your fifth Unique Selling Point (research and development testing facility).

> Mr. Jones, please. Hello, Mr. Jones. This is Susan Simms of Office Tech. How are you today? Great! One of the chief concerns we are hearing from others in your position is the need to test their technology solutions prior to purchase. Is this the same issue impacting your business, or are there other ones? [Mr. Jones responds.] Great! We have been very successful in helping companies like yours overcome issues very similar to these. I'm going to be in your area on June 25 and would like to stop by and introduce myself. Are you available at 3:00?

By employing this strategy, you will also be demonstrating perhaps one of the greatest qualities or virtues of professional selling: persistence. After all, the prospect is going to want to know that you will be there to follow up on the sale and support him through out the life of the purchase. As a professional salesperson, you must demonstrate that you will be there to support your customer after the sale, by showing strong, consistent, persistent, and customer-focused behavior prior to the sale.

If you reflect on what we have covered in this book so far, we have made some major progress. In Chapter 5, we talked about how to select the best prospects in the market (making every call a potentially quality call). Smart prospecting also taught us the intervals in between calls. We called this our "call cadence," and our call cadence was based on the priorities we established.

In Chapter 7, we developed our basic script. The basic script was to be used on your first call to the prospect.

In this chapter, we established our business-development strategy. The business-development strategy forms the foundation of our approach to prospecting. It shows us what to do after we make our first call to the prospect and are not successful. The business-development strategy shows us how to cultivate a prospect in a structured, consistent manner, always adding value into the prospecting process.

Our next chapter explores handling objections. Here, we will show you how to increase your chances of getting the appointments that we all desire.

FIGURE 8-15 Sample follow-up letter focusing on your fifth Unique Selling Point (research and development testing facility).

September 15, 20XX

Mr. Robert Jones
Director of Administration
NYT International
15 South Salem Avenue
Lower Newton Falls, MA 06000

Dear Mr. Jones:

It was a pleasure to speak with you today. I'm sorry that we were not able to get together. However, I did want to provide you with an example of how our customers use our research and development testing facility to help their business be more successful.

At Office Tech, we work with our customers to help them jointly develop, test, and implement their technology solutions. This allows our customers to know that the solutions they implement with us will help their organization become more productive. Given the size of your organization and your position within the industry, I thought our research and development testing facility might be of value to you. We are seeing a strong need for this type of service among our largest corporate accounts.

I have enclosed some information on our testing facility for your review, and I will be contacting you shortly to discuss your interest in this idea. In the interim, should you require additional information or have any questions, please do not hesitate to contact me.

Yours very truly,

Susan Simms
Account Manager

[Note: For an e-mail, you would leave out the formal heading or address. You might even want to address the person by his or her first name if this is the custom in your country.]

Handling Objections

Once, in a prospecting seminar at a franchise organization, I had just completed the "Anatomy of a Cold Call" segment, and someone from the Boston franchise raised her hand and said that all of this sounded fine to her, but in Boston, the calls don't always go as smoothly. Well, calls don't go that smoothly in New York (my hometown) either, or anywhere else in the world for that matter. The woman who asked the question was referring to the fact that her prospects don't always readily agree to meet with her. Rather, they provide her with reasons why they don't want to meet—that is, *objections*.

There are two interesting characteristics of objections. First, there are only a limited number of objections that you will come across in your selling career. This has tremendous implications! Since there are only a limited number of objections, we can plan for the objections and also plan our responses. Second, objections really aren't objections at all. They are simply a request by the prospect for additional information.

Assume that you are trying to set up a meeting with a particular prospect. Assume further that the prospect does not want to meet with you because of a particular reason. What the prospect is really telling you is that you have not provided him with enough information at this point to justify taking time out of his busy schedule to see you.

There is some tremendous synergy here. Since we can plan for the objections and respond to them by providing additional information, we should be able to turn around any objection with the same skill and ease that our prospects enjoy in sending them our way.

I have compiled what I believe to be a comprehensive list of objections. There are only seven objections on this list

I also provide you with a well-developed response or two to each objection. Like the basic script, my responses should be used for guidance. Your response should be consistent with your industry and personality. Only then will you continue to sound conversational.

Developmental Stages in the Learning Process

Before we actually address objections, I would like to provide you with one additional insight. Adult learners go through four stages of development in the learning process: unconscious incompetence, conscious incompetence, conscious competence, and unconscious competence. In the first stage—unconscious incompetence—the adult learner, or salesperson in our case, is not aware of what he doesn't know. Essentially, the salesperson is a newcomer to a particular skill.

During the second phase, the salesperson becomes aware of his lack of skills and is very concerned about the deficiency. In the third stage of development, the salesperson starts to become better at the particular skill set; however, he must constantly think about what he is doing in order to accomplish the task. In the fourth phase, he can perform the task extremely well, without thinking about it at all.

It is the unconscious competence stage that we are striving for in our cold-calling efforts. Both our script and our planned responses to objections must be reflexive on our part. The entire cold-call process lasts only two to three minutes, and you must be able to think and react rapidly during the entire call. The only way to reach this stage is to practice, practice, and practice.

Yes, I did say practice. Why learn on your real live prospects? Once you get someone on the phone, you'll have one opportunity, the two to three minutes, to get the appointment. You wouldn't want to get off the phone knowing that you could have done much better. It may be a year before you'll have the opportunity to speak with the prospect again.

I practice my prospecting script and responses in much the same way that I prepare for a speech. I go over the information again and again until I have it just right. Only then do I get on the phone and start dialing.

Famous Objections

The following is the list of objections that we plan to address:

❏ Send me information about your company/products/services in the mail or by e-mail.

❏ We handle the need for your product [service] internally.

❏ We have an existing relationship with a company like yours.

❏ I'm not the person responsible for this.

❏ We do not have the budget for your product or service.

❏ Your price is too high.

❏ We have used your company in the past and were dissatisfied.

Send Me Information About Your Company/Products/Services in the Mail or by E-Mail

In my experience, this response is one of the most commonly used objections. You reach a prospect on the phone, and he tells you to send some information in the mail or by e-mail. Most salespeople respond to this objection in a positive manner. They send the information as requested and believe that they have moved one step further in the sales cycle.

My experience, however, has been that in most instances, you are no further along in the sales cycle than you were prior to the call. Once you hang up the phone, the prospect is going to return to whatever he was doing. He is not going to spend much time, if any, reflecting on the brief discussion you just had. When he receives the information several days later or reads his e-mails several hours later, he may remember your discussion, but in all likelihood he will not.

It has been my experience that prospects use this objection to make the salesperson feel as though she has made a positive step in the sales cycle. The prospect can issue the objection without getting into a detailed discussion with the salesperson. This objection also minimizes the prospect's investment in the phone call.

Since this objection is extremely common, it is very important that you have a good response in your sales arsenal. I am going to give you two ways to respond to this objection. My responses are presented in Figure 9-1.

There are several interesting points here. Let's look at the first response I provided.

When you hear this objection, what you want to do is to drive the customer into the sales discovery process. In case you are not familiar with the sales discovery process, it is simply the process through which we learn about the customer's needs. We do this by asking quality, open-end questions.

In a normal discovery session, I would ask the customer six structured, high-level, open-ended questions. If you take a look at the response that I provided, it says, "What I would like to do is ask you a few more questions before I send the information."

FIGURE 9-1 Sample script responding to the "Send me information about your company/products/services in the mail or by e-mail" objection.

Response I: I'd be happy to send you information in the mail [or by e-mail], but we have a lot of different information to send. What I would like to do is ask you a few more questions before I send the information. That way, when I send the information, I will send you only what is relevant to you.

Response II: Since I've already sent you information, it must have gotten lost in the mail. I'm going to be in your area on March 16. Why don't I stop by at 3:00 and drop it off? Will you be available? Great! I'm noting this in my calendar and will call you the day before to confirm.

However, there is an important distinction here. If you are in field sales, the goal of your prospecting call is to get an appointment, not to do a discovery session over the telephone. This is the job of the tele-sales professional. So, while I am telling the customer that I would like to ask him a few questions, I really want to ask him only one question, the first question in my structured discovery process.

The question I would actually ask is "What are you doing now in the area of [insert your product or service]?" What I am doing here is asking the prospect how he currently handles his need for what I am trying to sell (and actually get the appointment to sell). While I do have five other planned questions to ask, my hope is that the prospect will tell me something that I can use as leverage for the appointment. So, after he responds, I could say something like, "Well, that's a really interesting point, and it just so happens that we have been able to help other customers in areas just like these. What I would like to do is discuss this with you in more depth. Are you available next Tuesday at 3:00?"

Now let's take a look at the second response I provided. This one is pretty clever.

Imagine that you are calling and calling, and almost every time that you call, the prospect says, "Send me something in the mail (or by e-mail)." If you get this response again and again, and you may, I suggest that you build this response into your basic script. So, instead of saying something like "One of the chief concerns we are hearing from others in your position is . . ." you could try something like "The reason I am calling is that I sent you something in the mail [or by e-mail]."

If you use a basic script like the one in the preceding paragraph, it makes it more difficult, but not impossible, for the prospect to say, "Send me something in the mail." After all, you just told the prospect that you already sent him something.

However, if he does happen to say, "Send me something in the mail" in spite of your revised basic script, you can use the second response indicated in Figure 9-1. In other words, you can use the prospect's statement about sending something in the mail as the very reason you need to have the appointment with the prospect.

There are two other points that I want to highlight with respect to this latter response.

First, the prospect can respond in one of only two ways. He can either agree to meet with you or he can provide you with an additional (real) objection that we will address later.

Second, notice I am asking the prospect if he will be available. I am not going to simply drop off the information. I could hire a messenger or send it through the mail if that is what I wanted to accomplish. I am going to have a meeting—and not a brief meeting, either. Very rarely, if ever, will these "drop off the information meetings" last less than one hour. In fact, these meetings are in every way the same as the ones that were planned by the prospect. Finally, I always call to confirm.

We Handle the Need for Your Product [Service] Internally

This objection tends to be a very powerful one because it appears to be difficult to overcome. After all, why would prospects buy from you if they already make what you are selling themselves? However, overcoming this objection should be no more difficult than any other. As always, the key lies in preparation.

If you refer to our "Core/Niche" diagram, presented in Figure 9-2, what you should quickly come to realize is that when a prospect tells you that the prospect company handles the need for your product or service internally, she is really saying that the company has filled the core need for your product or service itself. Keep in mind that had the company not filled the need for your product or service itself, one or more of your competitors might have gotten the business.

Therefore, this objection and the following objection—in which the prospect tells you that he is happy with the services of one of your competitors—are very similar objections. The strategy for overcoming both objections is also very similar.

Further, we already established that most prospects will likely be aware of their need for your product and will have likely found a stable source of supply. Therefore, this objection should not come as a surprise at all. Rather, in addition to the first objection covered in this

FIGURE 9-2 **"Core/Niche" diagram.**

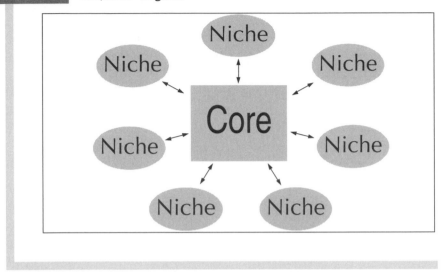

chapter, the internal and competitor objections are two of the most frequently used by prospects. I suspect that the three objections combined account for the majority of all objections you will receive.

Interestingly enough, the internal objection can also be handled in one of two ways. The way in which you handle the objection is a function of whom in the prospect organization you are working with: middle managers or upper managers. The responses are different because each classification of manager has a different set of interests or value system. Your response must be designed to reflect the interest of the party to whom you are talking.

Middle-Management Approach. An approach I like to recommend with regard to middle managers is to address one of their primary concerns: efficiency. Whatever they are doing is fine; you should just position yourself to help them do it better. This can easily be accomplished if we refer to Figure 9-2. Middle managers are typically proficient at addressing the core set of business needs. However, they typically do not have the capabilities, resources, or economies of scale to address, or cost-effectively address, niche needs. All organizations have niche needs or opportunities, and this should be the target of your comments. The approach of addressing niche opportunities is very unthreatening to a middle-management prospect because you are offering help by proposing to supplement her existing offering. You are not trying to take away her job by eliminating the need for what she does. My recommended response is presented in Figure 9-3.

After reviewing Figure 9-3, you might be wondering what you would do if the prospect asks you just how you can supplement her internal capabilities. This is where your Unique Selling Points come in. In Chapter 8, we outlined our Unique Selling Points and constructed a business development strategy around them. Any one of these Unique Selling Points could serve as a supplement to the prospect's internal capabilities.

For example, assume that you work for a company that sells plastic resins, and your prospect uses plastic resin in a variety of commercial and industrial applications. Assume further that the company is developing a new application and wants to test the application in a laboratory prior to full-scale production. The options are to build a testing facility for internal use or to rent a facility each time a new application must be tested. You just happen to call, and the prospect responds by giving you the internal objection. You reply with the script outlined in Figure 9-3. The company wants clarification on exactly how you can supplement its capabilities. Your answer is outlined in Figure 9-4.

Although this method might sound too good to be true, it works. You are trying to identify niche opportunities to supplement your prospect's strong internal capabilities. Any of your Unique Selling Points could provide a compelling reason to get together. I also recommend that you prepare a letter to send to the prospect to support your discus-

FIGURE 9-3 **Sample script for responding to the "We handle the need for your product [service] internally" objection—middle-manager approach.**

Great! That was exactly my reason for the call. We have worked with a number of large organizations like yours and have found that we can be an effective supplement to the services you already provide through your organization. I'm going to be in your area on August 5 and would like to stop by to show you how. Are you available at 3:00?

FIGURE 9-4 Sample script for adding to your response to the "We handle the need for your product [service] internally" objection—middle-manager approach.

> Ms. Jansen, recently our company opened a new research and development testing facility to support our first-to-market commitment. Not only does this facility support our internal research and development efforts, but we have also allowed our customers the opportunity to use our facility to test potential applications prior to full-scale production. We have found that many organizations like yours view this as a major benefit of doing business with us, and I thought it might be of value to you. I would like to stop by next Tuesday at 3:00 to introduce myself and share with you other areas in which we might be able to supplement your strong internal capabilities.

sion. A sample letter has been provided for your reference in Figure 9-5.

Upper-Management Approach. Middle managers are typically concerned with doing a better job. This makes their life easier and also allows them to perhaps progress to upper management. Our supplemental approach works well with middle managers because it helps them achieve their goal of doing a better job.

Upper management, on the other hand, is typically concerned with return on investment, earnings per share, and other broad-based financial performance ratios. Thus, your response to upper managers' internal objection should show them that you can increase the profitability of their company.

Before we craft our upper-management response, let us understand why we are so well-positioned to increase the profitability of a prospect organization that handles the need for your product or service internally.

First, economies of scale typically rest with you. Economies of scale say that you can produce the same product that they can, but you can do it more cost effectively. If you can produce the product more cost-effectively, then you are in a position to provide prospects with a lower total cost solution. (If you are not well-positioned to provide the

FIGURE 9-5 Sample follow-up letter for responding to the "We handle the need for your product [service] internally" objection—middle-manager approach.

July 30, 20XX

Ms. Sally Jansen
Director of Manufacturing
International Plastic Company
45 Roberts Drive
Kansas City, MO 66631

Dear Ms. Jansen:

It was a pleasure to speak with you today. As we had discussed, we have worked with a number of large organizations like yours and have found that we can be an effective supplement to the services you already provide through your organization.

For example, recently our company opened a new research and development testing facility to support our first-to-market commitment. Not only does this facility support our internal research and development efforts, but we have also allowed our customers the opportunity to use our facility to test potential applications prior to full-scale production. We have found that many organizations like yours view this as a major benefit of doing business with us, and I thought it might be of value to you. I would like to stop at your convenience to introduce myself and share with you other areas in which we might be able to supplement your strong internal capabilities.

I have enclosed some corporate literature for your review and will be contacting you shortly to reassess your interest in our company. In the interim, should you require additional information or have any questions, please do not hesitate to contact me.

Yours very truly,

Paul Robertson
Senior Account Executive

[Note: For an e-mail, you would leave out the formal heading or address. You may even want to address the person by his or her first name if this is the custom in your country].

prospects with a lower total cost solution, you can always use the middle-management supplementary response as your fallback position.) Hence, you can improve the profitability of their organization. Economies of scale typically rest with you because your organization is highly focused on the production of the product or service in question. Prospect organizations are in business to produce the product or service that they sell to their customers, and the production of your product or service is not the main focus of their attention. Accordingly, it stands to reason that you should be more effective at the production of your product or service than they are.

In addition to offering economies of scale, your organization typically services a broader base or population of customers than their internal population for your product. Their organizations serve only their internal customer base, while yours serves many organizations within your target market. You have a much larger base over which to amortize your research and development costs and spread your risks, so you can produce your products or services more cost-effectively.

One of the greatest risks facing organizations today is the risk of technological obsolescence. Products, services, and systems are changing at an ever-increasing rate, and an internal organization with a smaller customer base may not have the resources to justify a large investment in current technology. Your organization does. In other words, your organization offers a nice alternative when it comes to outsourcing the risk of technological obsolescence and outsourcing research and development efforts outside the target company's core competencies.

It is important when working with upper management that you be prepared to speak their language. Upper managers speak primarily a financial language. You are preparing to tell them that you can provide them with a lower total cost solution than the one they have in place. I am certain that they will be interested in your response, but I am equally certain that they will want you to justify your position. The ability to quantify the impact of your recommendation is crucial to your success with upper management.

In the training business, for example, many companies in our target market often find themselves discussing the alternatives of outsourcing the administration for their training program or handling the registration function internally. Typically, the internal registration function can be managed by one individual at an annual salary of $25,000 to $35,000. Using the average, let us assume that the internal registrar is paid $30,000 per annum.

In order to fully understand the outsourcing alternative, you must understand that a person's salary is only one element of the total cost of keeping a person on the company payroll. In addition to the person's salary, there are added costs of benefits, such as health care; overhead costs, in that you must provide the person with office equipment and a place to work; management time, since you want to provide the employee with an appropriate level of supervision; and inefficiencies, since you can count on the employee getting sick and you having to pay a temporary employee to replace the lost manpower.

These additional costs are known as a corporate burden rate. This rate is designed to reflect the total cost of employment for an organization, not just the cost of the employee's salary. The rate can range as low as 120 percent for many small companies to as high as 270 percent for many Fortune 2000 companies. I like to use the approximate average in this range of 200 percent, or twice the employee's salary. Continuing with the analysis, the registrar now has an internal cost to the organization of $60,000, not the $30,000 first contemplated.

There is one other important distinction. An employee is a fixed cost to a company—that is, you pay for the resource irrespective of usage. Assuming that you fully utilize the resource (for the 250 working days in a year), the daily internal rate for registration services would be $240 per day ($60,000 divided by 250 days in a year). If you use the resource to only 75 percent of its efficiency, your daily rate rises to $320 per day. Although this figure might not seem significant, a comparable rate for an outsourced event registration service might be $100 per day, or approximately 30 to 40 percent of your internal cost. The other big benefit in this analysis is that the outsourced resource is a strictly variable cost; you pay for it only when you use it.

This type of quantitative argument can be quite compelling and should be coupled with qualitative factors such as quality (we should be able to provide the service more effectively since this is our line of business), ease of administration (when employees call in sick, it is our responsibility to replace them, not yours), ease of recruitment (it is our responsibility to find qualified resources), and ease of doing business (the customer has one point of contact for all of her needs in a particular area). Having developed both the quantitative and qualitative elements of my analysis, I might respond to the internal objection as outlined in Figure 9-6 when working with upper management.

You begin with the trademark transfer of enthusiasm. The prospect has just told you that he doesn't need you because he can provide your product or service internally, and you are completely undaunted by his response. Further, the prospect is expecting you to be completely overwhelmed because he has just told you that he can do what you do by himself and you respond by saying that's exactly why you called. This leaves the prospect wondering exactly what you will say next. And what do you say? You explain that you can provide the company with a lower total cost solution, thus improving the profitability of the organization. Do you think that your prospect is interested? Of course he is! You then go for the appointment. This response works well for upper managers because it directly addresses their primary mandate: to increase the profitability of their organization. A letter to support your script and response has been included in Figure 9-7.

We Have an Existing Relationship

Before we cover this objection, it is important to note that this is probably the most difficult objection to overcome. This is also the objection that you are most likely to receive.

FIGURE 9-6 Sample script for responding to the "We handle the need for your product [service] internally" objection—upper-management approach.

Great! That was exactly my reason for the call. We have worked with a number of large organizations like yours and have found outsourcing to be a lower total cost solution to their needs. I'm going to be in your area on July 18 and would like to stop by to show you why. Are you available at 3:00?

FIGURE 9-7 Sample follow-up letter for responding to the "We handle the need for your product [service] internally" objection—upper-management approach.

July 5, 20XX

Mr. Michael Martinez
Chief Financial Officer
Farefront Corporation
222 Market Street
San Francisco, CA 91111

Dear Mr. Martinez:

It was a pleasure to speak with you today. As we had discussed, we have worked with a number of large organizations like yours and have found that outsourcing can be a cost-effective alternative. For example, recently our company was able to save another large organization more than $100,000 through outsourcing. We have found that many organizations like yours view outsourcing as a cost-effective alternative, and I thought it might be of value to you. I would like to stop by at your convenience to introduce myself and share with you details of our outsourcing alternative.

I have enclosed some corporate literature for your review and will be contacting you shortly to reassess your interest in our company. In the interim, should you require additional information or have any questions, please do not hesitate to contact me.

Yours very truly,

Paul Robertson
Senior Account Executive

[Note: For an e-mail, you would leave out the formal heading or address. You may even want to address the person by his or her first name if this is the custom in your country].

The reason that this is a difficult objection to overcome is that vendor selections are often accompanied by extensive research on the part of the customer. When customers make a vendor selection, they do so with the understanding that they have made the best selection that they could for their business.

When you encounter this objection, you run a significant risk of offending prospects because almost anything that you say, especially telling them why you and your company are better than their current vendor (which is often what salespeople do), essentially attacks their decision-making process. You must avoid attacking prospects' decision-making process at all costs.

Also, if you consider the nature of this objection, you should easily see why it is so commonly received. If you are prospecting, then you know that the company or individual that you are calling is not your customer. Therefore, unless you have a monopoly on your product or service, it is safe to assume that the account belongs to one of your competitors. Hence, the competitive objection. I would estimate that you will receive this objection about 80 to 90 percent of the time.

So let's take a look how we can overcome this difficult and frequent objection.

If you consider this objection, you should see that the prospect's telling you that she has an existing relationship with one or more of your competitors is no different from the response of prospects who handle the need for your product or service internally. An internal department or vendor is really no different from an external vendor.

Referring to Figure 9-2, the prospect is simply telling you that she has filled the core need for your product or service. Your goal, in this instance, should be to identify a niche, or unfilled need. The response outlined in Figure 9-8 is appropriate when you encounter this objection. A supporting letter is provided in Figure 9-9.

Should prospects question your ability to supplement their existing relationships, your Unique Selling Points will back you up, as they did when we encountered this objection in relation to the internal resources of the prospects. If you are lucky enough to know which of your competitors the target company is working with, you may want

FIGURE 9-8 Sample script for responding to the "We have an existing relationship" objection.

> Great! That was exactly my reason for the call. We have worked with a number of large organizations like yours and have found that we can be an effective supplement to the services already provided by your primary supplier. I'm going to be in your area on November 2 and would like to stop by to show you how. Are you available at 3:00?

to consider focusing your response to those Unique Selling Points that highlight your strengths vis-à-vis the competition.

Further, a prospect who is already using a competitor is, in many ways, better than a prospect that does not use your type of product or service at all. A company that already uses your type of product or service believes in the value of your industry. Your competitor has already done much of your work for you. All you have to do is identify your niche, earn the right to advance, and continue to move further through the sales cycle.

I'm Not the Person Responsible for This

Often, in trying to locate the person responsible for purchasing your product or service, you come upon incorrect contacts. This comes into play most often when you are doing your preliminary prospecting work with a new account, when you are using old data that may have come from the salesperson who preceded you, and when you work a list without contact names.

From experience, I know that not having a prospect's name or having the wrong name, as the case may be, is perhaps the most dreaded problem in all of selling. You not only have to cold call to get the appointment, but you also have to search for the name of the definitive decision maker. Most salespeople find this a difficult problem to overcome. However, if handled properly, it can be the most direct and effective route to take when prospecting. Here's why.

First, you have no preconceptions about the prospect. I'm certain that all of us have avoided contacts either because they were difficult

FIGURE 9-9 Sample follow-up letter for responding to the "**We have an existing relationship**" objection.

October 15, 20XX

Mr. William Goodman
Executive Vice President
Industrial Rivet and Washer Company
1010 Gills Lane
Nanuet, NY 10509

Dear Mr. Goodman:

It was a pleasure to speak with you today. As we discussed, we have worked with a number of large organizations like yours and have found that we can be an effective supplement to the services you already receive through your primary provider.

For example, recently our company opened a new research and development testing facility to support our first-to-market commitment. Not only does this facility support our internal research and development efforts, but we have also allowed our customers the opportunity to use our facility to test potential applications prior to full-scale production. We have found that many organizations like yours view this as a major benefit of doing business with us, and I thought it might be of value to you. I would like to stop by at your convenience to introduce myself and share with you other areas in which we might be able to supplement your primary provider.

I have enclosed some corporate literature for your review and will be contacting you shortly to reassess your interest in our company. In the interim, should you require additional information or have any questions, please do not hesitate to contact me.

Yours very truly,

Leslie Maserjian
Senior Account Manager

[Note: For an e-mail, you would leave out the formal heading or address. You may even want to address the person by his or her first name if this is the custom in your country].

to work with or because we had bad experiences with them in the past. What I found when I finally did call back was often these old contacts were no longer in the same position and I could start working with new contacts. Had I taken the time to verify my assumptions, I could have reduced the length of my sales cycle tremendously.

Second, I'm also sure that all of us have called on people who were not the decision maker for the product or service we were selling. However, because you thought the person was the decision maker, you kept trying, which can be a big time waster. Had you taken a few moments to verify your assumptions, you might have been quite a bit more effective.

When you have a list with no names, your expectations of success are not as high because you are starting from a position of limited information and strength. Just like the underdog in sports, you have very little to lose, so you go out and give it your best. Often, the result is a performance far above your standard abilities.

The first step in using a list without names is to take the list and rank the prospects according to the demographic factor that best defines your target market, as outlined in Chapter 5. By ranking your prospects according to the demographic factor that best defines your target market, you are sure to work with the highest-impact prospects first. This will, of course, lead to you maximizing your return on investment.

Then, call the general number for the prospect company in question. Try to reach a receptionist, operator, or assistant, and solicit that person's support in finding the person responsible for what you sell. If you were in this situation, trying to find the decision maker using a list without names, the conversation depicted in Figure 9-10 would be appropriate.

This approach is successful because you have taken the time to identify yourself. People are very reluctant to give information to strangers. Because you have taken the time to identify yourself, you have overcome the first hurdle in your path. Also, you are soliciting help, not making a demand.

When you solicit people's support, my experience has been that they respond in a positive manner. When you place a demand on

FIGURE 9-10 **Sample script for locating the proper decision maker in a company.**

Hello, this is Paul Goldner of the Sales & Performance Group. I was wondering if you could help me, please? [A long pause.] I was looking for the person responsible for sales education within your company. Do you know who that might be? [Person responds.] Great! Before you transfer me, I was hoping you could provide me with a name and extension in case we get disconnected. Thank you for your help.

someone, my experience has been just the opposite. Saying "I was wondering if you could help me, please?" is the most powerful element in the script and greatly increases your probability of success at this point. The long pause requires a response. When you think about it, what are the chances of someone refusing to help you? When possible, it is also important to get the name and phone number or extension of the person to whom you are being transferred.

Once you get transferred, you need to determine whether you have reached the proper person. The script outlined in Figure 9-11 will get you this information. If you have reached the appropriate person, you can move directly into your basic script. If not, apologize for the misunderstanding and ask to be directed to the correct person. I find that you are typically transferred to the correct party about 80 to 90 percent of the time. This estimate is no exaggeration and is why I said that this is quite possibly the best way to prospect. It is the shortest distance between you and the definitive decision maker at the target company.

Occasionally, you will come across an uncooperative receptionist. When this happens, you can change the general phone number to

FIGURE 9-11 **Sample script for verifying that you have reached the proper decision maker in a company.**

Yes, Ms. Smith. This is Paul Goldner of the Sales & Performance Group. How are you today? Great! The reason I am calling is that they transferred me to you and said that you were the person responsible for sales education at your company. [Pause and wait for a response.]

direct-dial an employee. For example, if the general corporate number is 867-5000, simply replace the final zero with a number, selected at random, between one and nine. In other words, instead of dialing 867-5000, dial 867-5005 and reach an unknown employee.

By selecting a number at random, you almost certainly won't reach the person you are looking for. Continue until you get a live person on the line. You know in advance that you are going to reach the wrong person, so be prepared for the conversation.

A second technique to get past an uncooperative receptionist is to make up a name, say Mary Jones or Bill Smith. The conversation with the receptionist should proceed along the lines outlined in Figure 9-12. If the receptionist is not aware of who handles the purchase decision for your product or service, simply ask to be transferred to the human resource or personnel department. Once again, proceed as suggested earlier for situations when you are addressing a wrong contact.

We Do Not Have the Budget for Your Product or Service

My first thought when encountering this objection is to reflect on the Selling Life-Cycle Paradigm. Remember, selling is a process and not an event. Given this long term view of the sales cycle, you cannot expect an immediate return from every client and prospect. However, since you are working within *your* target market, every call is a quality

FIGURE 9-12 Second script for locating the proper decision maker in a company.

Receptionist: Gordon Industries. How may I help you?
You: Bill Smith please.
Receptionist: I'm sorry, we don't have a Bill Smith working at this company.
You: Maybe you can help me. I used to work with Bill in the area of office supplies. I was wondering if you could direct me to the person responsible for that function within your company now.
Receptionist: Sure. Let me transfer you to Harry Stevens.
You: Thank you. You've been most helpful.

call and every prospect is a quality prospect. You cannot hurt yourself by developing an account within your target market, no matter how long the account cycle might be for the prospect. Given that a prospect did not properly budget for your product or service, now might be the best time to start building a relationship. If this is the case, you may want to consider the approach outlined in Figure 9-13. Your supporting letter is provided in Figure 9-14. Personal relationships are the strongest relationships, and this strategy will pay handsome long-run dividends for you.

A second approach that you may want to consider is to reflect on the fact that your objective, as a professional salesperson, is to improve your customers' profitability, not detract from it. You must ask yourself, "How can my product or service benefit the prospect?" You should be able to provide some concrete answers to this question. For example, will your product or service improve productivity? Will it decrease expenses? Will it increase the performance of the sales force? There are a number of ways in which you can be of great value to prospects. Once you have identified the benefits you bring to the table, you might respond as outlined in Figure 9-15.

Here, we are using a very popular sales technique. It is known as the "Feel, Felt, Found" or the "Repeat, Reassure, Resume" technique. The foundation of this technique is that one of the most powerful motivating forces supporting one's decision to buy or not to buy is the fear of failure. Your response tells prospects that there are others out there that are in exactly the same position, that they reacted similarly,

FIGURE 9-13 Sample script for responding to the "We have no budget" objection.

Ms. Chang, I understand that you may have current budget constraints. However, my goal is not necessarily to sell you something today, but rather, to build a lasting relationship. I'm going to be in your area on January 6 and would like to stop by to introduce myself. This way, when you do have a budget, I will be well-positioned to serve your needs. Are you available at 3:00?

FIGURE 9-14 Sample follow-up letter for responding to the "We have no budget" objection.

January 2, 20XX

Ms. Jacqueline Chang
Director of Purchasing
JEG International
10 South Street
Portland, OR 98811

Dear Ms. Chang:

It was a pleasure to speak with you today. While I understand that the time might not be right for you to make a purchase of this nature now, I did want to take the time to introduce you to our organization. Many organizations like yours have grown to be some of our best customers, and I would like to start building our relationship now.

I have enclosed some corporate literature for your review and will be contacting you in the future to reassess your interest in our company. In the interim, should you require additional information or have any questions, please do not hesitate to contact me.

Yours very truly,

Elissa Goldsmith
Senior Account Executive

[Note: For an e-mail, you would leave out the formal heading or address. You may even want to address the person by his or her first name if this is the custom in your country].

and that once the prospects understand the nature of the offer, they will likely feel differently as well. This powerful technique can be used to turn around many objections, whether over the telephone or in face-to-face sales meetings. The key to using this technique again lies in preparation. If the prospect asks just how you might be of value, be prepared to respond.

FIGURE 9-15 Second sample script for responding to the "We have no budget" objection.

> Ms. Chang, I can certainly understand how you *feel*. In fact, many of our best customers *felt* the same way as you did when we first called upon them. But, what they *found* when we started working with them is that we could really help them save money on the purchase of our products and services [or, we could really help them improve their over-all productivity]. I'm going to be in your area on June 25 and would like to stop by. Are you available at 3:00?

Your Price Is Too High

The all-important objection to price eventually surfaces in every sales situation. First of all, consider that if your price is truly too high, nobody would buy your product or service and your company would go out of business. In addition, price is a relative issue, not an absolute one. Your job, therefore, is to show that your product or service warrants the price you are charging.

When questioned about the price of a product or service, I try to agree with the prospect. I allow that we are not the lowest-priced organization on the market. We are well aware of that. On the other hand, we are not the highest-priced, either. In all likelihood, there will always be someone in the market with a higher price than yours, and there will also always be someone in the market with a lower price.

Your job is to establish value, not to discuss price. In fact, your customers should be in search of the lowest total cost solution, not the lowest price. The difference can be quite significant.

Consider the following tale as an example.

Assume that you have the opportunity to purchase one of two certificates of deposit. The first certificate costs you $100 and yields 5 percent. The second certificate costs you $500 and yields 15 percent. Which certificate would you prefer, the cheaper one or the more expensive one? The answer is always the same. You would rather purchase the $500 certificate because the more expensive certificate is worth the price. Your job is now to show that your product or service is worth the premium you are charging.

Taking this one step further, as I would expect any sophisticated buyer to do, you need to consider that the initial purchase price is only one element in the total cost of ownership of a product or service. For example, assume that you went to a store to buy a suit and there were two suits that caught your eye, one for $200 and a second for $300. You really have only $200 to spend. Which suit might be the more appropriate purchase?

At first glance, you might conclude the $200 suit would be better for you. However, if you examine the facts a little closer, you might reach a different conclusion. A typical suit may last you approximately two years under normal conditions. If the more expensive suit is of higher quality, it may require that you bring the suit to the cleaner once a month. The less expensive suit may need to be cleaned and pressed after each wearing or once a week. If it costs $10 to clean a suit, you can see that the total cost of ownership for the less expensive suit amounts to $1,240: the original cost of the suit ($200) plus the weekly cleaning bill over a two-year period ($1,040). The total cost of ownership of the more expensive suit amounts to only $540: the original cost of the suit ($300) plus the monthly cleaning bill over a two-year period ($240). As you can see, a close study of the facts may lead you to change your conclusion.

One of our clients makes extruders, which are extremely expensive pieces of equipment that melt little plastic pellets so the plastic can be used to coat a variety of products, including diapers and potato chip bags. An extruder costs anywhere from $500,000 to $5 million. The company I was working with was the oldest and most established company in the industry. However, it was suffering from severe price competition from a company outside the United States. Often, the overseas competition would price a "comparable" product at 40 percent less than my client's product. My client had to establish very quickly that the price of the product was only one small element of the total cost of ownership. Here's how he did it.

First, my client was the oldest and most established company in the industry. The company had been in business more than a century and produced machines that it had sold more than 25 years ago that

were still in operation. The company's nondomestic competition con-
sisted of smaller, thinly capitalized companies whose machinery was
lasting an average of only five to 10 years.

Suppose, for example, that my client had an opportunity to sell a
particular extruder for $1 million. The foreign competition might price
a "similar" product at, say, $600,000. Quite a difference! However,
my client's machines were lasting at least twice as long as the competition's. Thus, over a 20-year period, the competition's machine could
cost as little as $1.2 million if it had to be replaced only once (the best-
case scenario) and as high as $3 million if it had to be replaced six
times (the worst-case scenario). Which machine is truly the lower-cost
alternative?

To further support its argument, my client was more likely to be
able to honor its warranty because the nondomestic competition was
often thinly capitalized. In fact, many of the nondomestic competitors
went out of business after only a few years. As one would go out of
business, a new nondomestic competitor would pop up to take its
place. Prospects could see that if they were making an acquisition
priced between $500,000 and $5 million, they would want the company they bought the machine from to be in business long enough to
honor warranties and service the equipment. If not, they would be
faced with having to replace the entire machine, a costly alternative.

The third point that my client emphasized was the cost of servicing
broken equipment. Downtime for an extruder costs a company approximately $20,000 per hour. My client was able to provide next-day
parts and service whereas a non-U.S. competitor might take a week or
more. One breakdown a year would more than justify the price differ-
ential in the initial purchase.

Given the preceding examples, you might consider the response
to the price objection outlined in Figure 9-16. Figure 9-17 provides
your written response to the price objection. In order to close this call,
you would then quickly review your company's Unique Selling Points
as they relate to providing the target company with the lowest total-
cost solution.

A salesperson for the company that sells extruder equipment
needs to mention several elements that enter into the total cost of

FIGURE 9-16 Sample script for responding to the "price" objection.

Mr. Jackson, price is a concern to all of us. However, we work with a number of large organizations just like yours who believe that they receive an appropriate return on their investment with our company.

FIGURE 9-17 Sample follow-up letter for responding to the "price" objection.

June 12, 20XX

Mr. Steven Jackson
Purchasing Manager
Credit Card Incorporated
10 Wall Street
New York, NY 10001

Dear Mr. Jackson:

It was a pleasure to speak with you today. While I understand that you may have some concerns about our product pricing, I would still like to stop by and introduce you to our organization. Many companies shared your same concerns prior to fully understanding our product offering. In fact, many of these companies have grown to be some of our best customers, and I would like to start building our relationship now.

I have enclosed some corporate literature for your review and will be contacting you in the future to reassess your interest in our company. In the interim, should you require additional information or have any questions, please do not hesitate to contact me.

Yours very truly,

Jack Arthur
Senior Account Executive

[Note: For an e-mail, you would leave out the formal heading or address. You may even want to address the person by his or her first name if this is the custom in your country].

ownership of an extruder: the durability of the equipment, the stability of the organization, the company's ability to honor warranties, and the ability to provide timely service. The salesperson's close might be, "I'll be in your area June 23 and would like to stop by to discuss how these factors might enter into your decision. Are you available at 3:00?"

Your response should tell the prospect two things: first, that other organizations like his have felt that your services were worth the price you charge (remember Feel, Felt, Found); second, why you're worth what you charge (your unique selling points). Respond to concerns without getting into a lengthy debate over the phone. Commandment 3 advises you to keep your calls brief. Your goal is to respond as quickly and as efficiently as possible to each objection, then get the appointment. You will have ample opportunity in the face-to-face selling environment to establish value.

We Have Used Your Company in the Past and Were Dissatisfied

We hope that this objection is not encountered too frequently. If your company is doing a good job of servicing its customers, it will survive and prosper. If not, the market will tell you this, and your company will ultimately go out of business. The fact is that most companies that survive in today's increasingly competitive market do a good job of servicing their customer base most of the time.

However, mistakes do happen, and problems do arise. When they do, you must be prepared to respond. In fact, I would venture to say that most customers judge your company and you by the way you respond to adversity more than by the way you respond when things are going along smoothly.

When working with a dissatisfied customer, I like to rely on advice put forth by Dale Carnegie more than half a century ago. His principle for handling complaints is to "Let the other person do a great deal of the talking." This instruction is appealing because it is consistent with the ideal of consultative selling—to let the customer or prospect do most of the talking. Our role is to listen, take good notes, analyze the facts, and then make great recommendations.

Dale Carnegie thought that most people try to win others to their point of view by doing all the talking. His strategy was to ask the other person a question—the key element in the consultative sales process—and then let the aggrieved party explain what was bothering her. In short, his advice is to let the other person do most of the talking because she knows more about her problems (or needs) than you do.

A dissatisfied customer essentially has an unfilled need. So do all prospects! Your job is to immediately address the prospect and the problem (or need) head-on. An effective response to this concern is outlined in Figure 9-18.

As you can see, we are going to use the customer's dissatisfaction to gain the leverage required to get the appointment. The bottom line is that, when you get the appointment, you must rectify the problem *at any cost.* The reason is known as the "Law of 250," which states that each person knows 250 other people. Do something right for a person and she is likely to tell other people. Do something wrong to a person and she is sure to tell everyone she knows. The power of word of mouth is incredible. Think about the last new restaurant you went to. You probably went on the recommendation of a friend. Figure 9-19 contains your written response, if necessary. Remember, a dissatisfied customer represents a wonderful selling opportunity.

Can You Turn Around Every Objection?

These examples show that it pays to be prepared for objections. And let me show you one more way to prepare for objections. This is the great secret to objection handling that I referred to in the beginning of this chapter. Please refer to Figure 9-20.

As you can see, there are only four objections in all of sales, worldwide. This is true irrespective of your country or your industry.

FIGURE 9-18 **Sample script for responding to a dissatisfied customer or prospect.**

Ms. Jones, I'm glad I was able to get in touch with you. In fact, that is why I called. What I would like to do is stop by your office next Tuesday at 3:00 to learn more about your source of dissatisfaction. Then, I can start to take action to help you resolve your concern.

FIGURE 9-19 Sample follow-up letter for responding to a dissatisfied customer or prospect.

September 10, 20XX

Ms. Jori Jones
Sales Manager
ACME Tire and Tube
15 North Salem Avenue
Boston, MA 06000

Dear Ms. Jones:

   I am glad that I was able to speak with you today. I am very concerned about your perceptions and would like to stop by your office to better understand them. Zebra Systems is very proud of its products and will do whatever is necessary to support them.

   I have enclosed some corporate literature for your review and will be contacting you in the future to reassess your interest in our company. In the interim, should you require additional information or have any questions, please do not hesitate to contact me.

Yours very truly,

Taryn Keith
Senior Account Executive

[Note: For an e-mail, you would leave out the formal heading or address. You may even want to address the person by his or her first name if this is the custom in your country].

The first objection is the price objection. All of you know that price is likely to arise at some point in the selling cycle. When confronted with the price objection, you must respond with a value or total cost of ownership ("TCO") argument as outlined earlier.

The second objection is the competition objection. This objection refers to both internal and external competitors. Here, as noted, you must use the supplemental or complementary argument. There is almost no way around this.

FIGURE 9-20 Objection handling summary.

Price:	Competition:
■ **Objection** √"Your price is too high"	■ **Objection** √"We're happy w/current provider" √"We handle the need for your product/service internally'
■ **Responses** √Value √Total costs	■ **Responses** √Supplement √Complement
Will It Work?	**Not Now:**
■ **Objections** √"Just give me a reference acct." √"Used your company in past . . ." ■ **Response** √Use relevant customer references	■ **Objections** √"No need, interest, no budget" √"Send something in mail" ■ **Response** √Build rapport, enter discovery, close for appointment

The third objection is what I call "Not Now." This simply means that the prospect does not want to meet with you at this moment. As you can see from Figure 9-20, there are a number of ways that the prospect can state the Not Now objection. (In fact, that is true of all four objections. While there are a number of ways for the prospect to communicate an objection, it is important that you hear the objection, place it into one of these four categories, and respond in an appropriate manner.)

Returning to the Not Now objection, you try to build rapport by demonstrating empathy for the prospect's statement, then ask a question to try to rekindle the discussion and then go for your appointment based on the answer to your question.

The fourth and final objection is what I call the "Will It Work" objection. Here, the prospect is asking you, "If I buy from you, will the relationship be successful?" The only way to respond to a Will It Work objection is with reference stories. Of course, you can tell prospects about the virtues of your product, service, or company but that is what they expect you to do, and they place little value on an answer of this type. The true professional will always have a reference story in hand to demonstrate how she has helped companies like the prospect's overcome issues or challenges similar to the one that it is facing now.

Remember that objections are going to come, and, because there are really only four objections in all of sales, they should not overwhelm you. You can develop a simple, well-thought-out response to each of the four objections discussed.

Please note that our responses have substance as well as thought. When you actually analyze your response, you are helping make your customer or prospect better off. If you can help your customer or prospect become better off, you should be an evangelist for your product or service. You have nothing to be ashamed of and should aggressively pursue your business opportunities.

At this point, you might also be wondering if all objections can be overcome. The answer to this question is obviously "no." By preparing for objections, we are assisting you in developing thoughtful responses that will enhance your probability of success during the prospecting process. Remember, if the prospect doesn't want to meet with you, there is really nothing that you can do to change that. However, finding out this information (as soon as possible) is a positive event. Now you can properly position this prospect in your sales pipeline and focus the lion's share of your efforts on finding those prospects in your target market who are ready, willing, and able to buy now.

I always try twice on the same call to turn around the prospect's objections and get the appointment. After that, the conversation becomes strained and unnatural. Remember, you may want to call this prospect back again at some later date. In fact, you surely will. So don't burn any bridges. Once I have made two attempts on the same call to turn around the objection and have been unsuccessful, I simply tell the prospect that I will keep him on our mailing list and follow up at a later date to see if things have changed.

This tack does two things for you. First, it confirms the fact that the prospect is interested in your product or service. If the company has absolutely no interest, it will ask to be removed from the mailing list. Second, you open the door for your follow-up call, where you have some really great opportunities.

At this point, you made two bona fide attempts at getting the appointment and were unsuccessful. The question then becomes, What do you say on your follow-up calls? My experience has been that if you say or do the same thing, you will likely experience the same result—another rejection. I like to believe that the prospect did not give you an appointment on the first call because you did not uncover a need. Therefore, our approach to follow-up calls should be very similar to that outlined in the preceding chapter. The prospect needs to be placed in the Business-Development Cycle. This way, each time you call the prospect, you will be presenting him with a new reason to meet with you.

Your prospecting strategy, as it relates to overcoming objections, is presented in Figure 9-21. My first follow-up call relates to my first Unique Selling Point. Using our manufacturer of high-technology of-

FIGURE 9-21 Prospecting strategy for overcoming objections.

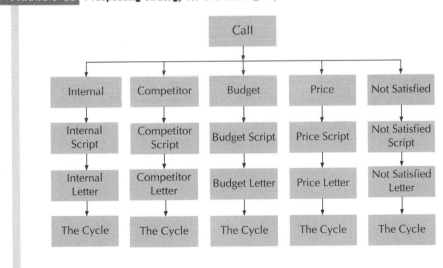

fice equipment, Office Tech, the conversation might proceed as indicated in Figure 9-22. In reviewing Figure 9-22, you should notice that this is the same script we presented in Chapter 8 with regard to Office Tech's first Unique Selling Point. The only difference is the introduction to the script, which reminds the prospect of the fact that you have already spoken and that you are following up on the prior conversation you had.

This approach yields excellent results. Typically, the prospect will not remember your initial conversation. However, since you are following up, the prospect will assume that he asked you to do so. Since this is your second call, he also realizes that he has put you off once already and it probably wouldn't be polite to do so again. Further, he assumes that since he asked you to call back, he must have a need for your product or service. You usually get the appointment. However, if you don't get the appointment, don't get emotional. Just schedule the prospect for an additional follow-up call and move on to your next Unique Selling Point.

Chapter 8 outlined the first element of our business-development strategy: what to do when you reach the prospect and get the appointment. This chapter outlined a strategy for overcoming the objections you might encounter in the business development and prospecting process. Chapter 10 is going to complete our strategy by outlining an approach to use when you do not reach the prospect you intended to call—in other words, what to do when you encounter voice mail or an assistant.

FIGURE 9-22 Sample script for your second attempt at penetrating a target account.

Mr. Jones, this is Susan Simms of Office Tech. How are you today? Great! The reason I am calling is that we had spoken back on September 15 and you had asked me to follow up with you at this time. As you may know, we were recently first to market with a new high-technology office system that will revolutionize the way companies do business. We have successfully installed this new system at a number of organizations like yours, and I would like to come by and demonstrate it to you. I'm going to be in your area on October 30 and would like to stop by. Are you available at 3:00?

CHAPTER 10

Working with Voice Mail and Administrative Assistants

This chapter brings our prospecting and business development strategy full circle. Chapters 7 and 8 discussed what to do when you reach the person you were intending to reach and get the appointment. Chapter 9 talked about overcoming objections—what to do when you reach the person you were intending to reach and do not get the appointment. This chapter outlines a strategy that will allow you to work with both voice mail and administrative assistants. You will learn techniques you can use when you do not reach the person you were intending to reach when you made the call.

Working with Voice Mail

When I wrote the first edition this book, in 1995, voice mail was a fairly recent introduction to the world of professional selling. Now it is pervasive. However, whether in 1995 or today, voice mail can be a great source of frustration for the sales professional.

Unfortunately, most salespeople have not developed a thoughtful strategy for how to respond to voice mail. It is often viewed as the ultimate gatekeeper. An alternative is to view voice mail as the ultimate advertising vehicle.

Voice mail gives you an unfettered opportunity to deliver a message. By unfettered, I mean that you can present your position without interruption or objection. In fact, this may be the only time in your life that you will have the opportunity to speak and not have someone present an alternative position.

Because you have an opportunity to speak without interruption, you need to have an approach or strategy prepared. In fact, you ought to have an advertising campaign prepared. Working with voice mail then becomes a matter of what to place in your advertising campaign.

Once again, your five Unique Selling Points will provide you with plenty of ammunition. These Unique Selling Points can be the basis for your company's voice mail advertising campaign. Each time you call the prospect, leave one of the following messages, in sequence:

First call: Introductory message

Second call: Message relating to Unique Selling Point number 1

Third call: Message relating to Unique Selling Point number 2

Fourth call: Message relating to Unique Selling Point number 3

Fifth call: Message relating to Unique Selling Point number 4

Sixth call: Message relating to Unique Selling Point number 5

The plan in working with voice mail is to immediately place your prospect in the Business-Development Cycle, as shown in Figure 10-1. Figure 10-1 is identical to the Business-Development Cycle that we presented in Chapter 8. However, here, we must slightly modify the contents of both our Unique Selling Point letters and scripts and also introduce a script for the introductory portion of the Business-Development Cycle. The modifications to your Unique Selling Points scripts and letters are minimal, so I have only recrafted one letter and one script to serve as an example. These are presented in Figures 10-2 and 10-3.

The introductory script and letter are based on your basic script and are presented in Figures 10-4 and 10-5. Please note that the intro-

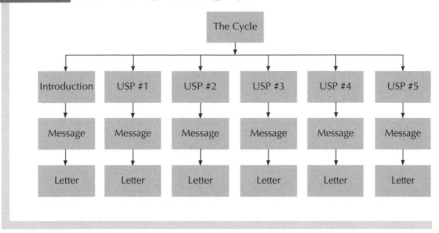

FIGURE 10-1 Business-development strategy reprise.

FIGURE 10-2 Sample script for first Unique Selling Point voice-mail message.

Hello, Mr. Jones. This is Susan Simms of Office Tech. The reason that I am calling is that we are hearing a lot of concern in the market about the need to have a company's office systems keep pace with its business needs and the needs of its customers. We have been very successful in helping companies like yours overcome issues very similar to these. I'm going to be in your area on June 25 and would like to stop by and introduce myself. Please give me a call at 212-555-1212 so that we may set up a mutually convenient meeting time. Thank you very much, and have a great day.

ductory voice-mail script is used on your first call to a prospect, when you reach voice mail.

It is important to reemphasize that this strategy gives you either 6 months, 18 months, or 36 months worth of voice-mail messages if you follow the callback periods recommended in Chapter 5. Further, the Business-Development Cycle is reusable in that when you reach the end of your first series of messages, you can simply go back to the beginning and slightly alter the focus of each of your original messages. After all, if your company was first to market with a product six

FIGURE 10-3 Sample follow-up letter for first Unique Selling Point voice-mail message.

February 20, 20XX

Mr. Robert Jones
Director of Administration
NYT International
15 South Salem Avenue
Lower Newton Falls, MA 06000

Dear Mr. Jones:

Recently, I gave you a call to introduce you to a new, high-technology office system that will revolutionize the way companies do business. This system has been shown to reduce total cost of ownership by as much as 20 percent in companies like yours. Given the size of your organization and your commitment to providing state-of-the-art products to your customers, I thought this new system might be of value to you. We are seeing a strong need for this type of solution among our largest corporate accounts.

I have enclosed some information on our new solution for your review, and I will be contacting you shortly to discuss your interest in this idea. In the interim, should you require additional information or have any questions, please do not hesitate to contact me.

Yours very truly,

Susan Simms
Account Manager

[Note: For an e-mail, you would leave out the formal heading or address. You may even want to address the person by his or her first name if this is the custom in your country].

months ago, you may have a new first-to-market product introduction the next time you need to use this Unique Selling Point message.

After you have left your carefully prepared advertising message on the voice mail of the decision maker, you may want to consider immediately calling back. This time, however, you are calling not to

| FIGURE 10-4 | Sample script for introductory voice-mail message. |

Hello, Mr. Jones. This is Paul Goldner of Sampson Management Company. We have not spoken before, but we have been working with companies in your industry for many years. One of the chief concerns we are hearing from others in your position is the need to improve the effectiveness of their management information systems. We have been very successful in helping companies like yours overcome issues very similar to these. I'm going to be in your area on June 25 and would like to stop by and introduce myself. Please give me a call at 212-555-1212 so that we may arrange for a mutually convenient time. Thank you very much and have a great day.

leave a message but rather to speak to the decision maker's assistant. Here, follow the strategy outlined in the following section. At a minimum, you want to make certain that you are addressing the proper decision maker.

When working with voice mail, there are several additional key ingredients, gleaned from the 10 Commandments of Prospecting, that will improve your chances of success: be persistent, vary your call times, try nontraditional hours, and always earn the right to advance. Your voice-mail advertising campaign should be supplemented by focused letters or e-mails, again bringing out your Unique Selling Points, corporate mailings, and handwritten notes highlighting articles of interest to the prospect.

Working with Administrative Assistants

Administrative assistants also seem to be a great source of frustration for many sales professionals. The key to working with administrative assistants is to understand their role in the sales process.

When you reach an administrative assistant instead of a decision maker, you must understand that what has changed is the level of the sale. You must still make a sale, however. Please consider Figure 10-6.

For purposes of this discussion, I am defining product and service sales as tangible transactions because they result in a physical transac-

FIGURE 10-5 Sample follow-up letter for introductory voice-mail message.

February 20, 20XX

Mr. Robert Jones
Director of Administration
NYT International
15 South Salem Avenue
Lower Newton Falls, MA 06000

Dear Mr. Jones:

Recently, I gave you a call to introduce you to our company. We provide high-technology office systems to large corporations like yours, and I would like to stop by and introduce myself. I have enclosed some corporate literature for your review and will be contacting you shortly to discuss your interest in our company. In the interim, should you require additional information or have any questions, please do not hesitate to contact me.

Yours very truly,

Susan Simms
Account Manager

[Note: For an e-mail, you would leave out the formal heading or address. You may even want to address the person by his or her first name if this is the custom in your country].

FIGURE 10-6 Different levels of a sale for working with administrative assistants.

Sale Level	Sale Type
Product or Service	Tangible
Appointment	Conceptual
Pre-Appointment	Conceptual

tion in which funds are exchanged in return for either goods or services.

Administrative assistants simply add a third level to the sales process. When you reach an administrative assistant instead of a decision maker, the nature of the conceptual sale changes. Instead of making the goal of your prospecting call to get an appointment with the decision maker, you must change the goal of the call to having the assistant allow you to talk to the decision maker.

The best strategy for reaching the decision maker is to work with the administrative assistant, not around him. The first thing I always do is ask the assistant his name. This can be tremendously flattering, especially when you consider how assistants are treated by many organizations and salespeople. Once I have learned the name of the assistant, I immediately record it in my contact management system. Thus, when I call back, I can immediately address the assistant by name.

I do not recommend investing time in setting up face-to-face meetings with assistants, since you can do some very effective work over the telephone. I have found most office assistants to be extremely knowledgeable in their supervisor's business affairs. In my business—the training business—the assistant would have a firm understanding of sales training.

When you reach an assistant, the conversation might go as depicted in Figure 10-7. Very often the assistant can provide you with a wealth of valuable information at this point. Always try to confirm the fact that the assistant's supervisor is the true decision maker for your product or service. I can't tell you how much time I've spent in my career chasing after people who were not the decision makers for my product. You don't get as many return calls as you would like when you are calling a person who has no interest in what you are selling!

Assistants can also tell you about their companies' current needs and future direction, which of your competitors it is using, and many other helpful pieces of information. After hearing the assistant's response and recording as much detail as possible in your contact management system, you can try one of several approaches.

First, assistants are often empowered to make decisions and appointments on behalf of their supervisors. If this is the case, the re-

FIGURE 10-7 Initial script for working with assistants.

Assistant: Mr. Venturini's office. How may I help you?
You: Mr. Venturini, please.
Assistant: I'm sorry, Mr. Venturini is in a meeting right now. May I take
    a message and have him get back to you?
You: Yes, this is Elissa Gabriel of Future Vision. Would you mind telling
    me your name, please?
Assistant: This is Adam.
You: Yes, Adam, how are you today?
Assistant: Fine.
You: I'm sorry, I didn't hear your last name.
Assistant: Smith.
You: Adam, the reason I'm calling is to follow up on the information I
    sent to Mr. Venturini. Our company provides duplicating services to
    large organizations like yours, and I just wanted to see how your
    company handles its needs for those types of services. Is Mr. Ventu-
    rini the decision maker in this area?
Assistant: Yes he is.
You: Great! Before I speak with Mr. Venturini, can you tell me a little bit
    about how you handle your needs in this area?

sponse in Figure 10-8 may be appropriate. Remember the movie *Wall Street*. It was the assistant who got Charlie Sheen his first appointment with Michael Douglas.

Unfortunately, not all assistants are willing to make an appointment for their supervisors. If this is the case, you might try the ap-

FIGURE 10-8 First supplemental script for working with assistants.

Adam, I'm going to be in your area next Tuesday at 3:00. The reason I
was calling is to set up an appointment with Mr. Venturini. Can you look
at his schedule and see if he is available at that time? He is? Great! I'm
going to put this appointment in my calendar. Would you please confirm
this appointment with Mr. Venturini and call me back to confirm? I'll
also call the day before to confirm as well. Thank you very much. I look
forward to meeting you next Tuesday.

proach outlined in Figure 10-9. We are both learning the best times to reach Mr. Venturini and trying to set up a telephone appointment. This will allow us to move to the second step on the sales ladder. In closing, you might also want to strongly consider leaving times that are best to call you back, to minimize the amount of telephone tag that you play.

If neither of the foregoing approaches work, you can consider the fallback position presented in Figure 10-10. Remember, if the assistant will not allow you to meet with or talk to the supervisor, your next best alternative is to change the level of the sale and see if you can first sell the assistant on letting you through to the supervisor. The key to this approach is not to think of assistant as just corporate gatekeepers. This has very condescending implications and can serve to increase the barriers between you and the true decision maker.

Assistants are there to help. They are there to help the person for whom they work, and they can be very helpful to you as well. Further, you never know where that assistant will wind up. Someday, he could be a decision maker at the company he presently works for or at another large organization. By winning the confidence of the assistant, you can work together to solve a common problem: how to get the decision maker and you together for a phone conversation or meeting.

If you are not successful, you can always refer back to the 10 Com-

FIGURE 10-9 Second supplemental script for working with assistants.

Adam, I'd like to speak with Mr. Venturini at a time that is more convenient for him. Is there a best time to reach Mr. Venturini? Would it be appropriate to set up a telephone appointment now?

FIGURE 10-10 Third supplemental script for working with assistants.

Adam, I have already sent our corporate literature to Mr. Venturini. What I'd like to do is send you a copy and then call you back to discuss it after you have had a chance to review this information. This will allow you to determine if it would be appropriate for me to meet Mr. Venturini.

mandments of Prospecting. First, remember to call at off-peak hours. Decision makers often work at times when assistants do not: 8:00 to 9:00 A.M., noon to 1:00 P.M., and 5:00 to 6:00 P.M. are great cold calling hours. Also, don't forget the "golden minute": 11:59 A.M. This is the single best minute to cold call during the entire day.

Second, remember to vary your call times. People are creatures of habit and are often doing the same thing at the same time, each and every day. By varying your call times, you will catch both the decision maker and the assistant at different moments in their daily and weekly routines.

Third, don't get emotional or discouraged. We are talking about a dial of the phone. It's up to you to be persistent, to keep on trying. If you are persistent, you will eventually get through.

Finally, your prospects are not sitting around waiting for your call. You must *earn the right* to work with your prospects. If you are having no luck on the telephone, consider sending a well-worded letter with some corporate literature. Overnight mail often has a greater impact than does regular mail. Faxes also work quite well. Keep your eye open for articles on your prospect's company. Clip the articles and send them to the prospect with a brief handwritten cover letter. Over time, these will surely earn you the right to advance.

We have spent the preceding chapters outlining a business-development strategy that will increase your probability of success in the sales cycle. There are two more ideas, however, that we can use to make us more successful: engage in practices that will make your prospects come to you, the subject of the next chapter, and learn from experience, the subject of Chapter 12. So, let's move on!

CHAPTER 11

Public Relations
How to Make Your Prospects Come to You

Thus far, we have worked exclusively with ideas that proactively help you penetrate a particular prospect within your target market. These ideas are crucial to your success and will certainly contribute to the probability of a positive outcome in the sales process. However, public relations tools, such as press releases, newsletters, public speaking engagements, and networking, can also be very powerful allies in your quest for selling success. A well-planned public relations campaign can position you as an industry expert and create excitement about what you do, building a mystique about you and your product. Opportunity will begin to chase you for a change.

Press Releases

When most people think of public relations, they think of both the cost and expense of hiring a public relations firm. Believe it or not, you can be your own public relations firm. All you need to begin is a list of names to send press releases to and a press release. Build your list of names with the definitive decision makers at your high-priority accounts. If you remember, a high-priority account in your target market is most likely to buy large quantities of your product or service.

You can also add local business and trade publications in your market, as well as producers of local television and radio shows.

Before we proceed with the press release discussion, I want to make one significant side point. It is based on something that we learned in Chapter 10 about working with administrative assistants.

If you recall our discussion, I strongly suggested that when you work with an administrative assistant you should always find out if that person's supervisor is the definitive decision maker. I do this even before I leave my first voice mail message. After all, why would you leave a message for someone who has absolutely no interest in receiving it?

So, when you first call to a prospect and get her voice mail, do not leave a message. First, press "zero" to get to her administrative assistant and confirm that her supervisor is, in fact, the person that you are looking for. Once you confirm this, you need to note this in your contact management or CRM system. There ought to be a field in your database called "DDM," for definitive decision maker.

If you are not sure if the person is a DDM, then leave the field empty. If you are sure that the person is a DDM, then place a "Y" in the field. This way, you can immediately filter your database of contacts for your confirmed DDMs. This will allow you to add focus and impact to everything that you do, especially in the public relations area.

Let's get back to our public relations campaign. In addition to your DDMs, make sure to send releases to the editors-in-chief of trade and business publications. The address of the editorial offices and the editor's name are always listed on one of the first pages of their publications. Releases should be sent to producers of shows that cover your industry on local television and radio stations. The producers' names are usually listed in the credits at the end of each show. Develop this list over time, and work to keep it current. The media industry is prone to change, and you want your list to be as accurate as possible. The information is all free and readily available.

Once you have compiled your list of accounts and media outlets, send one press release per month. More frequent mailings would dilute the effect of your release. Less frequent mailings would recall the old adage, "Out of sight, out of mind." Your release topics should be based on your Unique Selling Points and should be coordinated with your prospecting and voice mail activities.

To prepare press releases it is important to include these five key elements:

1. Your name, company, and address

2. The release date

3. The headline

4. The dateline (city of origin)

5. The body of the release

Keep your releases brief—one page if possible—and interesting. A sample press release announcing a new product introduction is presented in Figure 11-1. Please note that these releases can be sent via conventional mail or by e-mail. Both work, and both are effective. However, there are pros and cons to each approach.

The major benefit to e-mail is that it is essentially free. You don't have to pay for printing and mailing costs. The major detriment to e-mail is corporate spam blockers. Yes, the e-mail is free, but it may never reach the intended recipient. Snail mail incurs printing and mailing costs but isn't subject to spam blockers. (It is vulnerable to human blockers, however—people who screen the decision maker's mail.)

You have to weigh the merits of both approaches in your business and see which approach yields you a better return on investment over time.

Newsletters

Another publicity tool that works well is your own newsletter. If your company does this for you, that's great. However, if it doesn't prepare a newsletter, consider preparing one yourself and distributing the newsletter to the names on the list that you personally manage. Depending on the size of your mailing list, you may want to consider

Sample press release relating to one of your Unique Selling Points.

NEWS RELEASE

ABC Publishing Company
555 Cherry Hill Road
Port Charles, NY 55555

ABC Publishing Company
Exceeds the 1,000 Title Plateau

For Immediate Release
Thursday 22 September 1994

Contact: Jason Kaufman
914-555-1212

Port Charles—ABC Publishing Company (ABC), an international provider of innovative business titles, announced the release of its one thousandth distinct business title. The ABC titles span not only the conventional business publications such as sales, management, and personal development, but also include a full array of offerings in areas including team-building and excellence programs. "We take great pride in both the depth of our offerings as well as our first-to-market commitment," commented Jason Kaufman, ABC's CEO. "We believe that the combination of these two offerings uniquely positions us to service corporate America."

Founded in 1923, ABC Publishing Company is dedicated to providing the highest-quality business publications in the world. ABC's publications are designed to raise productivity, efficiency, and total quality by increasing employee effectiveness.

sending your newsletters to all the names on the list or to just a selection of key contacts—or what I referred to earlier as definitive decision makers. A newsletter can be a very effective device for positioning you as an industry expert, the value of which cannot be overestimated. I prepare my own quarterly newsletter to promote my sales training and speaking activities, and it has been well worth the investment in time.

Newsletters can also be sent via direct mail or e-mail. Again, e-mail is typically more cost-effective but you may want to weigh the benefits of direct mail versus e-mail in terms of getting your message through to the people you are sending it to.

Providing information to your clients and prospects is one of the ways you can add value to your product or service. The complexity of your product or service and the rate at which your product or service changes only serve to make information more and more valuable to your clients over time. Purchasers of goods and services are always looking to improve their position as a result of a purchase decision. Through a newsletter, the salesperson can provide useful information, helping the purchaser maximize the value received from your product.

A newsletter also gives you the opportunity to reach out to many prospects at the same time and build your reputation as an expert and source of valuable information. However, publishing a newsletter is a time-consuming process, so prepare to publish only on a quarterly basis. Anything more might prove to be too burdensome, and anything less would probably dilute the impact of your efforts.

Your newsletter activities should be coordinated with your press releases. During the months that you mail your newsletter, it's best not to send a press release. You do not want to inundate people with too much information at once. If you do, they will tend to get overloaded and probably not digest much, if anything, of the message you delivered.

If you still print a newsletter, your newsletter should be no more than four $8^1/_2$ -by-11-inch pages. Print each newsletter on both sides of one sheet of 11-by-17-inch paper, so it can be folded in half and read like a book. This is much neater than stapling pages together. When you choose the paper for the letter, check that it is thick enough to print on both sides without words showing through. Four pages provide enough space for one or two focused articles. The articles should be brief and to the point. They should also provide the reader with one or two nuggets of valuable information. Most people already have a tremendous amount of information they must absorb. I try to give them something extremely valuable that they can absorb in a very brief time frame.

Be sure to keep the information fresh and current. Our company has been sending newsletters for almost 10 years now, and over the years I have gotten calls from prospects who were on our mailing list and consistently received our newsletter. The message was always the same: "Thank you for keeping me on your mailing list. After five years of receiving your newsletter, I finally saw something that might be of value to our company. When can we get together?"

That's correct! Definitive decision makers at large organizations called us to do business! The newsletter had finally struck a chord. Once you begin your newsletter, keep sending it. The impact you will create over time will be tremendous. Earlier you read about a man trying to break a rock with a sledge hammer. Ultimately the cumulative effect of the blows broke the rock. A newsletter works in the same manner. Its cumulative effect can be very powerful.

Public Speaking

Following on the theme of reaching out to many prospects at once, public speaking can be a powerful supplement to your sales activities. Speaking in public, like professional selling, is a skill that can be mastered by anyone. Toastmasters International, an organization dedicated to improving your communication and leadership skills, is an excellent option to anyone interested in improving her speaking skills. The opportunity to speak in front of several hundred decision makers in your industry should be seized. Industry conferences are always hungry for speakers. All you have to do is develop a topic of interest and volunteer.

Start at the smaller conferences, and fine-tune your speech and your skills. Then move on to the major conferences in your industry. Besides increasing your sales opportunities, you'll get to travel and will have fun. The result of your presentations will be inbound requests for additional information. If you reflect on just how hard it is to get an appointment with a prospect, a healthy supplement of inbound requests can be very refreshing. Once you obtain a speaking engagement, refrain from selling your goods and services while on the platform. Focus on providing valuable information to your audience. The sales will follow.

Networking

Some might think that networking is an obvious recommendation and not worthy of mention in this book. However, networking can take place at two levels: the obvious and the not so obvious. The obvious form of networking is to network within the industries of your clients and prospects—in other words, to network within your target market. The benefit of this type of networking is that it establishes you as a player in the industry, gives you industry visibility, and allows you to meet the other players in the industry—your colleagues, as well as your prospects. The negative aspect of this type of networking is that you always meet the same people, and all of them have their guard up. In other words, they expect you to sell! This preconception can be difficult to overcome.

Networking outside your target market can be very powerful. This is one additional advantage to membership in Toastmasters, for example. Because the focus of a Toastmasters club is personal development, not the sale of your product or service, the opportunities that tend to develop are more real and immediate. Country clubs, health clubs, civic organizations, volunteer groups, charities, and other similar organizations can provide an additional source of prospects and sales opportunities.

Prospecting and business development are hard work. This chapter was devoted to taking the "chill" out of cold calling by providing you with some ideas to supplement your direct business-development activities. The next chapter focuses on the final element of our core strategy: leveraging your success with existing customers to help you find new customers and prospects.

CHAPTER 12

How to Leverage Your Success

The first eleven chapters of this book outlined an approach to business development and prospecting that can be employed by anyone, even if it is your first day in sales. Ultimately, however, you will make a sale, and this chapter will teach you how to leverage your success to create additional sales opportunities. The key to this approach is to have an existing customer for whom you have performed well endorse your product or service.

An endorsement is the use of one person as a reference for the credibility of another. We see this all the time on TV. Companies pay millions of dollars to have movie, television, and sports stars endorse their products. The reason they do this is that people assume that if the famous person uses the product, it must be good enough for ordinary folks like them.

In professional selling, we can also use an endorsement to enhance the probability of our success in the sales cycle. The value of an endorsement is almost immeasurable. In fact, I always say that an endorsement is the most powerful selling tool that there is. After all, the prospect expects you to say good things about your product or service. In fact, many prospects do not lend much credibility to our use of superlatives with respect to our company, our products, and our services.

However, prospects do give a lot of credibility to a third party, one with no vested interest in the sale of your product or service, who gives you an endorsement. As I noted, this is the most impactful selling tool that there is. In fact, since the third party receives no financial remuneration as a result of the endorsement, a third-party endorsement in the context of professional selling may have even greater impact than the types of endorsements we are used to seeing on television. No amount of selling on your part can equal the value of even the smallest endorsement from a third party in the eyes of a prospect.

Third-party endorsements can be testimonials from customers inside the target prospect. An endorsement from inside the target prospect organization is perhaps the most powerful endorsement there is. Here, you are doing work in one area of a company. Assume that it is the pension area. You have just successfully completed a project, and you ask the definitive decision maker in the pension area if he is aware of anyone else in the organization who could use your product or service.

Since you have just successfully completed a project, the likelihood that the company will give you a reference is quite high if the company is aware of someone with a similar need. If you are referred to another individual within the organization, your cold-calling script might look like the one in Figure 12-1.

In reviewing the script, you will of course notice that the script

FIGURE 12-1 First sample script for a "third-party endorsement."

Mr. Weineib, please. Hello, Mr. Weineib. This is Jacqueline Jencine of Maughan Industries. How are you today? Great! The reason that I'm calling is that we just completed a very successful program for your company in the pension area. We were working with Arlene Gersh.
Our company provides a financial information database to large organizations like yours, and Arlene thought that you might have a need for this type of information. How do you handle your needs for this type of information in your area? Great! I'm going to be in your area on May 31 and would like to stop by and introduce myself. Are you available at 3:00?

does not vary much from the basic script presented in Chapter 7. This script, and the endorsement approach, has particular power because each successful company has its own quality standards and any vendor it uses must meet or exceed those quality standards.

By virtue of the fact that you have successfully completed a similar project in another area of the company, you have exceeded the requisite quality standard. Thus, the risk for the new prospect in the sale is greatly reduced, and he is more likely to move forward. In other words, your chance of making a sale with an existing customer is far greater than with a former customer or with a cold call. I always say that "it is easier to sell more of your product or service to the same company or individual than it is to find new companies or individuals to sell your product or service to."

Endorsements from outside the organization of your prospect can also be valuable sales tools. Suppose, for example, that you worked with a large brokerage firm and recently completed a successful project. You can now use this experience to open the door at other brokerage firms. A potential script is presented in Figure 12-2. Once again, use the basic script, but with one minor modification: Use your past success to help you get the appointment. If you think about it, as long as you have completed one successful program at any company, you could try the third-party endorsement approach with other prospects. You will find that it will work quite well for you.

The final type of endorsement is the general third-party endorsement. I first discovered this tool when I was working in the mammoth corporate parks of New Jersey. Since New Jersey is quite spread out, it

FIGURE 12-2 Second sample script for a "third-party endorsement."

Mr. Davids, please. Hello, Mr. Davids. This is Teresa Smith of Exel Brokerage Services. How are you today? Great! The reason I'm calling is that we just completed a very successful project for Merrill Lynch. In fact, we provide brokerage services to many large organizations like yours. How do you handle your needs for those types of services at your company? Great! I'm going to be in your area on June 2 and would like to stop by and introduce myself. Are you available at 3:00?

is not uncommon to visit four accounts in a day and put 200 to 300 miles on your car. Any salesperson in this territory must learn to make the best use of his time. What I found is that when I went to visit an account, there were often other large organizations either in the same corporate park or in the same general vicinity. Most salespeople had a tape recorder in their cars and recorded the location of the account for later follow-up. I developed a more efficient approach, using third-party endorsements.

To start, walk into the offices of the other accounts unannounced and go up to the receptionist. Your discussion might proceed as outlined in Figure 12-3. This approach is similar to using a list without names and has just about as much success. It is a very effective method for learning the name of the definitive decision maker. You can follow up several days later for an appointment.

A similar approach can be used at smaller branch offices of larger organizations, or even at smaller companies, as long as they are in

FIGURE 12-3 Face-to-face "third-party endorsement" script.

Sales rep: Hello. My name is Paul Goldner of The Sales and Performance Group. I was wondering if you could help me.
Receptionist: Sure.
Sales rep: Our company provides sales training to large companies like
   yours. In fact, we provide sales training to many of the major com-
   panies in the area. I was driving by and just happened to notice
   your company. I was wondering if you could tell me who would be
   responsible for purchasing sales training in your organization.
Receptionist: Sure. That would be Mr. Travers.
Sales rep: Thank you. You have been most helpful. As long as I am here,
   I was wondering if you could do one other small favor for me.
Receptionist: Sure. What can I do to help?
Sales rep: I was wondering if you could deliver this package to Mr.
   Travers.
Receptionist: Why not?
Sales rep: I'm sorry, but I didn't ask your name.
Receptionist: Sally Smith.
Sales rep: Sally, you've been most helpful. Thank you.

your target market. Here, the conversation would go exactly like the preceding one, except that you might ask the receptionist to distribute your product literature to everyone in the office. This is particularly important if everyone in the office could use your product or service or if you are trying to develop an overall awareness for your product or service. Try this latter approach if the office houses 50 employees or fewer.

Receptionists in small offices tend to be very helpful. Be certain to note the receptionist's name because this, you hope, will be the beginning of a long relationship. Go back periodically to distribute product literature. Until you can develop a firm relationship with a true decision maker, this individual will be your internal champion, to represent your cause when you are not there.

Third-party endorsements represent an excellent opportunity to leverage your success at a particular account and to leverage your success as a salesperson. At this point, we have outlined an in-depth strategy for prospecting, cold calling, and business development. The final step in the process is to learn how to effectively track our progress, the subject of the next chapter.

CHAPTER 13

Tracking Your Progress

The final element in your sales success formula is tracking your progress. Tracking your progress is important to your overall success, because if you track your progress, you can fine-tune your approach and your plans along the way. Sales reporting will allow you to understand your respective strengths and weaknesses. However, as we all know, sales reporting has both pros and cons.

Arguments Against Sales Reporting

I will immediately concede that sales reporting is time-consuming. The classic argument against sales reporting is that it takes away from valuable selling time. Although this may be true, sales reporting can also be a valuable coaching tool (for yourself and your manager) and a tool for strategic and tactical planning.

I prefer to view sales reporting as an investment in my own success. Sales reporting ensures that you are working smart. Sales reporting also requires attention to detail, a skill that is not a staple characteristic of most salespeople. Without this attention to detail, you may overlook many items that are vital to your success.

For example, assume that you continue to make call after call and never reach the decision maker you are targeting. A well-defined sales reporting form will identify this trend and tell you that you may want to consider changing your source of leads.

The final argument against sales reporting is that it can be complicated. There is a simple response to this. Difficulty in completing a sales report is typically a function of the form. If the sales reporting system is complicated, work with your manager or your company to make it simpler!

Arguments Supporting Sales Reporting

Now that we have reviewed, and, we hope, overcome, some of the negative elements of sales reporting, let's take a look at some of the benefits, including identification of areas for improvement and sales forecasting. As far as I am concerned, the pros far outweigh the cons, making sales reporting a skill worth learning to do well.

Perhaps the most pervasive benefit of sales reporting is that it can be used to help you improve the quality of your prospecting efforts. A well-developed (prospecting or weekly) sales report can help you understand your personal relationship among dials, completed calls, appointments, proposals, and, ultimately, sales. These performance trackers in turn indicate, for both management and yourself, opportunities for improvement.

Chapter 2 established the very valuable relationship between dials of the telephone and income. Figure 13-1, again, outlines these relationships. Please note that the relationships implied in Figure 13-1 are for illustration purposes only, though I have seen them borne out for many of our clients.

Your exact relationships depend on your industry, the list you are

FIGURE 13-1 Information from a weekly sales report, reprise.

Dials	Completed Calls	Appointments	Proposals	Sales	Sales $
100	50	13	13	5	$20,000

using for your cold calls, and your cold-calling prowess. The only way you can determine your exact relationships is by keeping track of your cold-calling activities over a long period of time. However, for illustration purposes, suppose that 50 percent of dials should lead to completed calls, but your ratio is only 25 percent. What does this mean? It could mean that you are not using a good or current list in your cold-calling efforts. It could also mean that you are not calling at a good time, and you may want to consider another time or varying your call times. The crucial point is that sales reporting can be a valuable feedback mechanism that will help you operate at peak performance.

Sales reporting can also help you (or your company) predict future demand for your product or service.

It is no secret that salespeople are not fond of preparing sales forecasts. Since sales forecasts create accountability, the salesperson may be required to live up to his projections. If salespeople are required to live up to their projections, they may tend to underestimate their capabilities. This way they are sure to meet their plan. However, if you follow this tack of consistently underestimating demand, you will not provide management with the necessary information to allocate resources and make capital expenditures.

In other words, it is in your best interest to accurately estimate demand so that you receive enough resources to meet the demands of your accounts. There is nothing as frustrating to a salesperson as selling an order and not having the product in place to meet customer demand. Accurate sales forecasts will help management to project demand for your product or service and have sufficient inventory or resources in place to meet the needs of your customers. Of course, you don't want to be overly optimistic in your projections, either. Here, management will overallocate resources, and the company will wind up making bad investment decisions. Nobody wins when the company makes bad investment decisions.

Sales reporting also helps you monitor goal attainment. As I mentioned earlier in this book, I am an avid Weight Watcher. I lost a lot of weight on the program, and over the years, I noticed one very interesting phenomenon. When I knew I would be going to Weight Watchers on Sunday morning in order to get weighed, I was religious about the program during the week. Consequently, I lost weight. On weeks when I knew that I would be out of town and would miss the dreaded Sunday morning weigh-in, I deviated from the program and usually gained weight. The point is, what gets measured gets done. What doesn't, gets forgotten.

In addition, when things are going well, one always has the tendency to pull back and smell the roses. The problem is that when you are smelling roses, someone else is working with your accounts and prospects. Weekly record keeping keeps your challenges alive, because each week you start with a clean slate. The likelihood of slacking off will be greatly diminished.

A final benefit of measuring your results is that it will help build your cold-calling confidence by proving that you make money each and every time you dial the telephone and that you have the ability to set your own level of income.

Your Sales Tracking Form

To record your sales prospecting activities, use a weekly sales tracking form such as the one presented in Figure 13-2. The form has five key segments: prospecting activity, meeting activity, pipeline activity, sales activity, and other pertinent information. The key elements of this form are the following:

Dials   Here you record how many times you dial the phone in order to reach a decision maker for your product or service. Please note that we are measuring dials of the phone, not completed calls (discussed next). The important thing to note is that dials are fully within your control, whereas completed calls are not. What this tells you is that the effort you put into the sales process, and your related sales success, is fully within your control. If you are not meeting your sales objectives, you can always increase your sales effort by increasing your dials.

(text continues on page 192)

FIGURE 13-2 Sample weekly sales tracking form.

XYZ Company
Weekly Sales Report

Prepared by: _____   Date: _____

Prospecting Activity:

Day	Dials	Completed Calls	Appoint-ments	Recommen-dations	Sales	Sales Dollars
Monday						
Tuesday						
Wednesday						
Thursday						
Friday						
Total						
Percent*						

*Calculated as percent of previous column.

FIGURE 13-2 Continued.

Meeting Activity:

Client	DDM	Date	Objective	Achievement	Stage of SC

DDM = Definitive Decision Maker. SC = Sales Cycle.

Pipeline Activity:

Client	Magnitude of Opportunity	Expected Close Date

Sales Activity:

Week	Weekly Sales	MTD Sales	Monthly Goal	% of Goal
One				
Two				
Three				
Four				

MTD = Month to Date

Other Pertinent Information:

_____

_____

_____

_____

_____

_____

_____

_____

_____

_____

_____

_____

Completed Calls	Here you record the number of times that you reach the person you are dialing. This includes callbacks, as well as times when you call the prospect and leave a message and the prospect calls you back and reaches you on the call (yes, this really does happen!).
Appointments	Here you record the number of appointments you receive from your completed calls.
Recommendations	Here you record the number of proposals you issue as a result of your appointments or meetings. There are two important points here. First, please note that the proposals you issue this week will come from meetings and calls that you scheduled or made weeks or months ago. Do not be concerned about this, because, over the long run, you will be able to see the relationships that we are trying to develop in this chapter. Second, please note that a proposal is simply an offer made by you that the customer can acknowledge and purchase. It can be written or it can be verbal, as long as the customer can say "yes" and purchase something from you.
Sales	Here you record the number of winning proposals you issue. Again, the sales that you make this week will come from activities in prior weeks. Over time, this will average out, and you will learn about your prospecting ratios, one of the major reasons for completing your sales reports.
Sales Dollars	Here you record the dollar value of the sales from the previous column.
Total	Here you record the sum of all the activity in each column for the week.

Percent   Use this row to establish the weekly relationship between your various sales activities. In the Dials column, record the percentage of dials that were completed calls. In the Completed Calls column, record appointments as a percentage of completed calls. In the Appointments column, show proposals as a percentage of appointments. Finally, include the percentage of proposals that resulted in sales in the Recommendations column. Over time, these ratios will normalize, and you will have a very reliable predictor of your sales activities.

By way of example, the ratios for Sara Jones might appear as presented in Figure 13-3. Consider using these results as target ratios for your cold-calling activities. If you are not able to achieve the same results as Sara's, you may need to make some changes in your approach.

For example, every two times Sara dials the phone, she completes one call (50 percent). If your rate is lower, consider changing your list or the times at which you make your calls. To improve your appointment ratio, you need to work on your telephone skills. Review the 10 Commandments of Prospecting and your cold-calling scripts. You should always strive to issue a proposal or set of recommendations after every meeting. A prospect is meeting with you because she has a

FIGURE 13-3 Sample business-development benchmarks.

Dials	Completed Calls	Appointments	Proposals	Sales
2	1			
	4	1		
		1	1	
			2–3	1

need. Your job is to uncover the need and develop a solution. Therefore, your ratio of meetings to proposals should be close to one-to-one. The proposal need not be a long and detailed document. A one-page letter might be sufficient. However, make certain you offer the prospect something she can purchase.

In our example, Sara makes one sale for every three proposals she develops. Although this result may be different than what you can expect in your industry, to improve your results, consider seminars in consultative selling and/or proposal writing. You need to increase your understanding of the customer's needs and more effectively present your recommendations.

Finally, consider how these overall numbers can help you plan your cold-calling strategies. Extrapolating from our example, you can see that it should take 20 dials of the phone to make one sale. Further, you should be able to make these 20 calls in one hour. Therefore, if you want to make one sale per day, you need to prospect one hour per day. To increase sales production, you must increase your prospecting production. The relationship is that simple.

Over time, you will develop a feel for your sales ratios. You can also learn about your sales skills relative to those of your co-workers by comparing your ratios to theirs. I don't know if sharing sales ratios is common practice in your office; however, it is quite beneficial to all who participate. In this manner, you can develop company and industry norms and have all members on the sales team strive to equal and exceed those norms.

The second and third components of your sales tracking form are used to track Meeting Activity and Pipeline Activity (see Figure 13-2). Your planned meeting activity results in your future sales or future income. If your inventory of appointments or opportunities runs too low, you can surely expect to have an income drought sometime in the future. Pipeline activity is designed to measure your imminent sales. These are significant sales that you should expect to close in the near future. The next segment, Sales Activity, measures your sales production on both a weekly and a monthly basis. The final portion of the form, Other Pertinent Information, is designed to reflect additional information that you believe is important to management or yourself and that is not captured in other areas of the report.

Save your weekly tracking reports. When you are going through a strong period of high sales, look back and review your prior prospecting activity. Likewise, if you are going through a period of slower sales, look back and see why. In both cases, reflect on the Law of Sowing and Reaping. Our prospecting success formula started with techniques for overcoming the fear of rejection, followed by the development of a number of strategies to enhance your probability of success in the sales cycle, and ended with methods for tracking your progress. The only question that remains is: Will this formula work specifically for you? That is the subject of our Conclusion.

Final Thoughts
The Four Steps to Success

The Four Steps to Success are a simple goal-attainment formula: Set goals. Have confidence. Be persistent. Have fun! This system will ensure that the recommendations set forth in this book work for you.

Step 1: Set Goals

In very simple terms, the need for goal setting can be summarized in one short sentence: If you don't know what you are shooting for, how are you going to hit your target? When you are setting your goals, set your sights high—extremely high. And don't fret if you don't reach your goals on the first try.

If you don't reach your goals today, you'll come back tomorrow and try again. Never give up. Further, as you try harder and harder to move outside of your comfort zone, even your failures (that is, those times when you don't reach your goals) will exceed the successes of most others. As goal setting relates to prospecting and business development, strive to be the very best you can—the best in your industry. As you set your goals, reflect back on Chapters 4 ("Becoming Rejection-Proof") and 5 ("Smart Prospecting").

Step 2: Have Confidence

When I teach my Four Steps to Success seminar to inner-city high school kids, I always start the session with one question: Who wants to be a success? The answer is always the same: a 100 percent positive response. Everyone wants to be a success. I go around the room and find that some of the kids want to be great athletes, others want to be show business personalities, others want to be the president of their country, and still others want to be doctors and lawyers—all very admirable goals, indeed.

However, when I ask how many think they can achieve their life's ambition, I always get a disappointing 10 to 20 percent positive response. I then tell a story of an experience that I had 30 years ago, when teaching this very same seminar in Little Rock, Arkansas (the home of the former President of the United States, Bill Clinton).

The session in Little Rock started just the same as every other seminar, by my asking the kids, "Who wants to be a success?" Just as I find today, I received a 100 percent response. As I went around the room and asked the kids what they wanted to be when they grew up, the answers were the same: doctors, lawyers, and stars of stage and screen. Believe it or not, there was a little kid in the class, Bill, who proudly declared that when he grew up, he wanted to be president of the United States.

As expected, all of the kids laughed at Bill. However, when you think about it, his ambition to be president of the United States was not as farfetched as it might have seemed at the time. Each generation must produce its leaders. As long as someone has to do the job, why shouldn't it be you? Have the confidence to live your dreams. In developing your dreams, to be the best salesperson in your industry, reflect on Commandment 9 (see the end before you begin or see yourself being successful).

Step 3: Be Persistent

It's very simple to look at a successful person and think how easily that person's success was achieved. However, most of us take the same road to success: hard work, many failures, and much persistence. The author Napoleon Hill said, "Within every failure is the seed of an equal or greater opportunity." Further, he noted that most great successes in life occur just after one's greatest defeat. Truer words have never been spoken.

Perhaps the greatest success story that I have ever read is the story of Victor Frankl, a prisoner in a Nazi death camp for many years. His book, *Man's Search for Meaning,* teaches the true meaning of persistence. Victor Frankl was able to endure the horrors of the Nazi death camps because he was motivated by the dream of being reunited with his family at the end of the war. It's amazing what one person can endure, yet so many of us want to give up after far smaller defeats. As business developers, our greatest challenge is only to overcome telephone rejection. Persist—and remember Commandment 10 (Don't Stop).

Step 4: Have Fun

The great secret of prospecting is also the secret to life's success. *Have fun!* That's it. While most people dread prospecting, you shouldn't. Learn to love it. Prospecting is not work; it's play. You must enjoy doing something in order to do it well. How do you think great athletes feel about playing their sport? I bet I can guess the answer to this question no matter whom you ask. Remember: Have fun.

Bibliography

Carnegie, Dale. *How to Win Friends and Influence People*. New York: Pocket Books, 1990.

Covey, Stephen R. *The Seven Habits of Highly Effective People: Restoring the Character Ethic* (15th anniversary edition). New York: Free Press, 2004.

Frankl, Victor E. *Man's Search for Meaning: Revised and Updated*. New York: Pocket Books, 1997.

Hill, Napoleon. *Think and Grow Rich*. New York: Ballantine Books, 1987.

Karasik, Paul. *How to Make It Big in the Seminar Business, Second Edition*. New York: McGraw-Hill, 2004.

Mackay, Harvey. *Swim with the Sharks Without Being Eaten Alive: Outsell, Outmanage, Outmotivate, & Outnegotiate Your Competition*. New York: HarperBusiness Essentials, 2005.

Index